# The Beginning of the Gospel of Jesus Christ

## HOMER A. KENT, JR.

BMH Books
Winona Lake, IN
www.bmhbooks.com

Mark: The Beginning of the Gospel of Jesus Christ

Copyright © 2005 by Homer A. Kent, Jr.

ISBN: 0-88469-246-9

09 08 07 06 05 04   6 5 4 3 2 1

Published by BMH Books
BMH Books, P.O. Box 544, Winona Lake 46590 USA
www.bmhbooks.com

Unless otherwise noted, all Scripture references are from the NEW
AMERICAN STANDARD BIBLE ®, Copyright © 1960, 1962, 1963,
1968, 1971, 1972, 1973, 1975, 1977 by The Lockman Foundation. Used by
permission.

Scripture references marked NIV are from the Holy Bible, New International
Version ®. Copyright © 1973, 1978, 1984 International Bible Society. All
rights reserved throughout the world. Used by permission of the International
Bible Society.

Scripture references marked KJV are from the Holy Bible, King James Version.

Interior design: Angela Duerksen
Editorial team: Jesse Deloe, Michaela Dodd, and Laura Bloomingdale
Typesetter: Grace College Art Department

Printed in the United States of America

# DEDICATION

To my six grandchildren
who make me very proud

Carrie, Brian, Kylie, Keegan, Madison, and Marshall


*"Children's children are a crown to the aged"*
—Proverbs 17:6 NIV

# ILLUSTRATIONS

All photographs are by the author.

# CONTENTS

# PREFACE

These studies in Mark's Gospel began thirty-five years ago as contributions to *The Brethren Teacher*, a Sunday school teacher's quarterly for 1969. They consisted of comments on selected portions of Mark, but were not a complete commentary on the entire Gospel. Some years later that material was republished in a new format with some revision as *Studies in the Gospel of Mark* (BMH Books, 1981). Now the opportunity has come to rework that volume, edit and reformulate many of the paragraphs, expand its contents to cover the complete text of Mark, and organize the material into a commentary on the Gospel.

Many years of teaching New Testament at Grace Theological Seminary have provided the background for these studies. Classroom interaction with eager students helped to sharpen my understanding of the biblical text, and has kept my love for the message alive.

Special thanks are extended to Jesse Deloe for his editorial work on this manuscript. His many helpful suggestions have made this a better book.

The intention in this volume is to explain the message of the Gospel as Mark presented it. This book will not deal at length with such matters as the origins of the Gospels (the Synoptic Problem), or with complicated technical data of interest mostly to scholarly researchers. It will pay attention, however, to parallel accounts in the other Gospels that help in the understanding of Mark.

This volume is designed for Bible students and classes for which there is interest in understanding the contents of Mark, without becoming bogged down with technical matters. Although the Greek text was open as this volume was written, references to that text are made only when they are important for understanding Mark's intent. It is my hope that Mark's Gospel may become clearer and its special features noted by those who may use this modest volume.

Homer A. Kent, Jr.
Winona Lake, Indiana
May 2005

# 1

# INTRODUCTION AND OPENING EVENTS
## Mark 1:1–13

The importance of the four Gospels to Christianity is incalculable. The Gospels furnish the only trustworthy account of the life of Jesus Christ. Jesus Himself wrote no documents. Only in the canonical Gospels do we find the true portrait of the historical Christ.

The Gospels, however, were not the first of our New Testament books to be written (the Epistles have this distinction). As long as the people who had been with Jesus were still living, there was no great need for written records. But as the message of Christ spread far beyond the land of Israel, the need arose for trustworthy accounts of His life and teachings. As the first century reached its midpoint and beyond, the deaths of the eyewitnesses were increasing; soon there would be no one who could verify from his own experience the truthfulness of the stories that were being circulated by word of mouth. Thus, the Gospels came into being, filling the need of the Church for all time. Although there seems to have been many fragmentary accounts in circulation (Luke 1:1–2), after the four Gospels appeared there is no indication that the early church showed any tendency to accept other documents as authoritative for the life of Christ apart from the four that we have today.

Mark's Gospel has not always received the attention from Bible students that it deserves. Some scholars have accorded it special treatment because of their theory that it was the earliest of the four and provided the literary basis for the others,[1] but often its message has not been carefully studied. The Gospel of Matthew is longer, and its treatment of Christ's discourses is much more extensive. Luke's Gospel is written from a Gentile point of view, which makes his work especially attractive to the majority of Christian readers. The Gospel of John, with its emphasis upon Christ's deity, has found much use. Mark, however, has often been overshadowed. This volume will be devoted to the message of Mark, noting the portrait of Christ that this important Gospel presents.

## Authorship of the Gospel

Even though the author is not named in the Gospel, from the earliest times, testimony to Mark's authorship is strong and abundant. In the second and third centuries such writers as Papias, Irenaeus, Clement of Alexandria, and Origen all asserted this fact. The earliest record that we have comes from Papias (around A.D. 130–140), who wrote, "Mark, indeed, having been the interpreter of Peter, wrote accurately, howbeit not in order, all that he recalled of what was either said or done by the Lord."[2] This seems to mean that Mark wrote in Greek the content of Peter's preaching,

---

[1] It is beyond the scope of this volume to examine in detail the various theories of the literary origins of the Synoptic Gospels, but rather to concentrate upon the text and interpretation of Mark's Gospel. For a careful analysis of current thinking about literary origins, see Robert L. Thomas and F. David Farnell, *The Jesus Crisis* (Grand Rapids: Kregel, 1998), and R. L. Thomas, *Three Views on the Origins of the Synoptic Gospels* (Grand Rapids: Kregel, 2002).

[2] Papias, as recorded in Eusebius, *Ecclesiastical History*, Book III, 39, 15.

which may have been originally given to Aramaic-speaking audiences. Or it may mean that Mark "interpreted" in the sense that he set down in writing and thus made widely available what Peter had taught. At any rate, Mark's Gospel was understood as being based on the personal experiences of the apostle Peter.

Another early notice comes from Irenaeus (around A.D. 180), who wrote, "After their decease [Peter and Paul], Mark, the disciple and interpreter of Peter, he also transmitted to us in writing the things which Peter used to preach."[3] Clement of Alexandria (A.D. 190) stated: "When Peter had publicly preached the word at Rome, and by the Spirit had proclaimed the gospel, that those present, who were many, exhorted Mark, as one who had followed him for a long time and remembered what had been spoken, to make a record of what was said; and that he did this, and distributed the Gospel among those that asked him."[4] Thus even though Mark was not one of the twelve apostles, the Gospel that bears his name is based on Peter's apostolic knowledge and is fully entitled to our acceptance as worthy of a place in the New Testament.

## The Man John Mark

Mark is not mentioned by name in any of the Gospels, and it is not certain that he appears in any of the narratives. Some have suggested that he was the young man who followed Jesus at the time of His arrest (Mark 14:51–52),

[3]Irenaeus, "Against Heresies," Book III, 1, 2, as recorded in Eusebius, *Ecclesiastical History,* I, 153.
[4]Clement of Alexandria, as recorded in Eusebius, *Ecclesiastical History*, Book VI, 14, 6.

since this could have been the author's way of including himself in his Gospel. The incident appears nowhere else, and there seems to be no other reason for mentioning the fact, as it has no importance in the narrative. It has also been argued that perhaps the Last Supper was held in the upper room of Mark's parents' home, since this was apparently a somewhat regular meeting place for Christians following the Resurrection (Acts 12:12). Greater detail is given in Mark's Gospel regarding the Upper Room than in the other Gospels.

Some details of Mark's career are known with certainty from Acts and the Epistles. Mark left his home in Jerusalem (Acts 12:12) to accompany Paul and Barnabas on the first missionary journey (Acts 12:25; 13:5). This was a somewhat natural arrangement, since he was a kinsman of Barnabas (Col. 4:10). Mark left the missionary party, however, after they arrived in Perga, and this defection made Paul unwilling to take him on the second journey (Acts 13:13; 15:37–38). As a result, Mark went with Barnabas to Cyprus on a separate tour (Acts 13:39). Some years later, however, friendship between Paul and Mark was fully restored (see Col. 4:10 and Philem. 1:24). When Paul was in his final imprisonment in Rome, he desired to have Mark join him there (2 Tim. 4:11). Part of Mark's ministry was spent as an associate of Peter (1 Peter 5:13), a fact corroborated by a number of historical notices previously cited. This man, from his rich and varied experience, authored our second Gospel by inspiration of the Holy Spirit.

## The First Readers

A number of early traditions connecting this Gospel with Peter also point to Rome as the place of writing and as the intended destination of the document. Certain features of the book itself indicate that it was written for a Gentile audience and that these Gentiles may have been Romans. Clement of Alexandria stated that Mark wrote while Peter was preaching at Rome.[5]

Mark frequently interprets Aramaic words for the benefit of his non-Jewish readers (see 5:41; 7:34; 10:46; 14:36; 15:22). He explains the location of the Mount of Olives more explicitly than most Jewish readers would have needed (13:3). The strong possibility that these Gentile readers were Roman is seen in Mark's usage of a number of Latin words not found in the other Gospels ("executioner," 6:27; "pitchers," 7:4; "cent," 12:42; "centurion," 15:39, 44–45), as well as some Latin words shared with the other Gospels.

Another reason for thinking that the Gospel of Mark was first written for Roman Christians is its mention of Simon of Cyrene as the father of Alexander and Rufus (15:21). Mark is the only Gospel to note this relationship. Mark must have mentioned it because his readers knew these men, and we know from Romans 16:13 that Rufus lived at Rome with his mother.

We do not presently have the data for a precise dating of the book. Irenaeus (A.D. 180) said that it was written after Peter's death.[6] This would give a date around A.D. 65–70, following the Neronian persecution but prior to the destruction of Jerusalem.

[5]Ibid.
[6]Irenaeus, op. cit.

## Distinctive Features of Mark's Gospel

Mark has the smallest amount of material of the four Gospels that is not shared with at least one other Gospel. Estimates vary slightly, but only about sixty-five verses of Mark cannot be found also in the other Gospels.[7] To some, this suggests that Mark was written first and was later expanded by the other writers. Many, however, see in this feature merely an independent production written for a different audience.

Mark spends very little time with the preliminaries of Christ's ministry. He tells us nothing of Jesus' birth and childhood. A sentence or two is all he devoted to the baptism and temptation. He confines himself to action, without much record of extended discourse. The word "immediately" occurs forty-one times ("straightway" in the KJV). He seems clearly most interested in the deeds of Jesus.

One of the greatest textual problems in New Testament studies concerns the last twelve verses of Mark's Gospel. The vast majority of Greek manuscripts contain all twenty verses of chapter 16. However, the two oldest uncial manuscripts, Vaticanus and Sinaiticus, end with 16:8. The same is true of the Old Latin codex Bobiensis, the Sinaitic Syriac manuscript, about one hundred Armenian manuscripts, and the two oldest Georgian manuscripts. Furthermore, Clement of Alexandria and Origen show no knowledge of these verses, and Eusebius and Jerome say that the passage was absent from almost all Greek copies of Mark known to them.[8]

---

[7]Scroggie, W. Graham, *A Guide to the Gospels* (London: Pickering & Inglis, 1948), 189.

[8]For more discussion, see Bruce M. Metzger, *A Textual Commentary on the Greek New Testament* 2nd Ed.(Stuttgart: United Bible Societies, 1994), 102–106.

Complicating the problem is the fact that some manuscripts have a shorter ending following 16:8. This ending states: "But they reported briefly to Peter and those with him all that they had been told. And after these things Jesus Himself sent out through them, from east to west, the sacred and imperishable proclamation of eternal salvation." Most of the manuscripts containing the shorter ending follow it with verses 9–20.[9]

The longer ending (16:9–20) is found in the vast majority of manuscripts, although not in the very earliest ones. Uncial manuscripts containing it are A, C, D, K, W, and many others. The earliest patristic evidence for it is Irenaeus in the second century. Bible readers are so familiar with this longer ending for Mark that any efforts to delete it are usually met with strong resistance. However, it must be recognized that the documentary support for it is not as strong as one could wish.

There are four possible explanations as to the ending of Mark: (1) the original ending by Mark has been completely lost; (2) Mark ended his Gospel at verse 8; (3) the shorter ending is the original one; or (4) the longer ending (vv. 9–20) is the original one.

One's choice would seem to be one of the following: First, Mark's Gospel ended at 16:8. Although it seems abrupt, it is not impossible, nor is it inconsistent with Mark's style of conciseness and quickly ending one discussion and moving to another. It does seem strange that Mark would end his Gospel on such a discouraging note. It has been suggested that perhaps he died suddenly at this point, and friends published the unfinished work with verses 9–20, just as someone other than Moses finished the book of

[9]Ibid., 103.

Deuteronomy in order to record his death (Deut. 34:5–12). If Mark originally ended with verse 8, this would account for the addition of the shorter ending, because if Mark always had verses 9–20, it is hard to imagine a reason for anyone to replace it with the less specific and generally colorless short ending. The shorter ending; however, has far too little documentary support to merit serious consideration as the original ending. To suppose that the original ending has been completely lost has no historical support and takes no notice of God's work of preserving the Scriptures.

Or, second, one might conclude that Mark's Gospel always contained the longer ending (16:9–20). The contents are consistent with the data found in the other Gospels, and no serious questions are posed by the information it contains. As long as it is recognized that its documentary support does raise serious questions, one may certainly use this portion of the Gospel as profitable and enriching of our understanding of those early days. No basic doctrines are conveyed in these verses, and therefore the problem is more relevant to textual scholars than to practical usage.

## Structure and Outline

After a very brief mention of John the Baptist's ministry and Christ's baptism and temptation, Mark goes immediately to Galilee and follows the career of Jesus in that northern province. No reference is made to earlier ministries in Judea, or to the visits to Jerusalem that Jesus made for various Jewish feasts. Mark does not contradict those activities; he simply ignores them. His basic format consists of Christ's Galilean ministry, a final journey to Jerusalem, and then the events of the Passion Week.

In light of the early historical references, which relate Mark's Gospel to the preaching of Peter,[10] it is interesting to examine the content and order of Peter's preaching at the house of Cornelius: "Jesus of Nazareth, how God anointed Him with the Holy Spirit and with power, and how He went about doing good, and healing all who were oppressed by the devil; for God was with Him. And we are witnesses of all the things He did both in the land of the Jews and in Jerusalem. And they also put Him to death by hanging Him on a cross. God raised Him up on the third day, and granted that He should become visible" (Acts 10:38–40). This order of events is precisely the pattern that is followed in the Gospel of Mark.

I. Opening Events, 1:1–13
  A. The Title, 1:1
  B. Christ's Forerunner, 1:2–8
  C. Christ's Baptism, 1:9–11
  D. Christ's Temptation, 1:12–13

II. The Galilean Ministry, 1:14–9:50
  A. Preaching and Teaching in Galilee, 1:14–5:43
    1. Call of Four Disciples by the Sea, 1:14–20
    2. Casting Out a Demon in Capernaum, 1:21–28
    3. Healing of Peter's Mother-in-Law and Others, 1:29–34
    4. First Tour of Galilee, 1:35–39
    5. Healing of a Leper, 1:40–45
    6. Healing of a Paralytic in Capernaum, 2:1–12
    7. Call of Levi, 2:13–17
    8. Discussion with the Pharisees and Others, 2:18–3:6

---

[10]Papias, op. cit.; Irenaeus, op. cit.

3. The Third Visit, 11:20–12:37
  a. The Withered Fig Tree Explained, 11:20–26
  b. Questioning of Jesus in the Temple, 11:27–12:37
    (1) Questioning by Jewish Leaders and the
      Parable of the Wicked Vine-Growers,
      11:27–12:12
    (2) Questioning by Pharisees and Herodians,
      12:13–17
    (3) Questioning by Pharisees and Sadducees,
      12:18–27
    (4) Questioning by a Scribe, 12:28–34
    (5) Christ's Question about David's Words,
      12:35–37
4. Denunciation of the Hypocritical Rich and
  Commendation of a Poor Widow, 12:38–44
B. The Olivet Discourse, 13:1–37
  1. The Setting, 13:1–4
  2. Future Events Prior to the "Abomination of
    Desolation," 13:5–13
  3. Future Events Following the "Abomination of
    Desolation," 13:14–23
  4. The Return of Christ, 13:24–27
  5. Warnings to Watchfulness, 13:28–37
C. The Final Hours, 14:1–72
  1. The Plot, 14:1–11
  2. The Last Supper, 14:12–26
  3. Prediction of the Disciples' Failure, 14:27–31
  4. Events in Gethsemane, 14:32–42
  5. The Arrest, 14:43–52
  6. The Jewish Trials, 14:53–65
  7. Peter's Denials, 14:66–72

# The Message of Mark

### The Title, 1:1

The opening words are really the title of the book: "The beginning of the gospel of Jesus Christ, the Son of God."[11] Mark regarded the public ministry of Christ as composing the beginnings of the Christian faith. If the assumption is true that Mark largely based his writing on the preaching of Peter, then the proclamation of the good news about salvation through Christ is certainly an appropriate understanding of the word "gospel" here. Mark was not using the term "gospel" in the specialized sense of a book, which the term later came to have in Christian circles (for example, the Gospel of Mark, Gospel of Luke, etc.).

---

[11]Although the words "the Son of God" are omitted in the 4th century codex Sinaiticus, they do appear in the equally old Vaticanus, as well as in D and W and most other manuscripts. It seems best to regard the omission from Sinaiticus as a scribal error of omission.

**Opening Events, 1:2–13**

*Christ's Forerunner, vv. 2–8.* Two passages from the Old Testament are cited to show that the coming of Messiah, and of one who would precede him, was clearly part of the divine plan. Malachi 3:1 predicted the coming of a messenger who would announce Messiah to the nation. Isaiah 40:3 predicted that Messiah's coming would be prepared by a spiritual working in men's lives rather than by a political revolution. Mark mentions only one of the original authors, Isaiah, a practice not uncommon among ancient writers when quoting from a combination of several sources (compare Matt. 27:9–10, where a composite quotation from Zech. 11:12–13 and Jer. 19:1, 6, 11 is attributed only to Jeremiah).

John, the son of Zacharias, is shown to be the fulfillment of these prophetic passages. All four Gospels relate the Isaiah passage to him. The mention of "all the country of Judea" and "all the people of Jerusalem" as coming to be baptized by John should be understood as a legitimate use of literary hyperbole. As he forcefully issued his call to repentance and performed a baptism in water upon those who responded, John was using a rite that was not entirely unknown to Jews. Converts to Judaism were required to undergo baptism. However, in such cases it was self-administered and was, furthermore, an initiatory rite. John's baptism, on the contrary, was in acknowledgement of a need for purification. It did not represent admission to a new society but symbolized repentance and cleansing from sin. Its distinctive purpose was new and God-given (Mark 11:29–32).

John's clothing recalls the garb of Elijah (2 Kings 1:8) and may have been purposely adopted to suggest the similar nature of their ministries. The camel's hair cloak was not a hide but woven cloth made from hair. Locusts and wild honey were a diet accessible to him in this wild country, but were not unknown in Palestine generally. The eating of locusts was specifically permitted in Old Testament law (Lev. 11:22). William Hendriksen has remarked, "Those who enjoy shrimp, mussel, oyster, and frog-leg should not find fault with those who eat the locust."[12]

As John preached, he clearly disclaimed any identification of Himself as Messiah. He showed that he and Messiah were on vastly different planes, even more so than a servant and his master. Furthermore, John's baptism was an external rite, symbolic and preparatory, even though it was the evidence of true repentance. But Christ would perform the full and final spiritual operation of regeneration by baptizing with the Holy Spirit.

*Christ's Baptism, vv. 9–11.* Mark's description is much briefer than Matthew's (Matt. 3:13–17). He does not explain the reason for this event, nor does he recount the conversation between John and Jesus. He is content to state the action.

As Christ emerged from the water, the Holy Spirit in the bodily shape of a dove descended upon Him. This was, among other things, an anointing of Messiah for His messianic work (Luke 4:17–18, Isa. 61:1–2). It also served as a sign to John (John 1:33).

The Father's voice gave the divine approval of Christ as one who pleased God in all things. Perhaps there is particular reference at this time to the previous thirty years of His life, which had fully pleased the Father.

The word "immediately" in verse 10 is the first of Mark's forty-one uses of this term.

---

[12]Hendriksen, William. *Exposition of the Gospel According to Mark* in New Testament Commentary series (Grand Rapids: Baker, 1975), 39.

*Christ's Temptation, vv. 12–13.* Mark's account is by far the briefest of the Synoptic Gospels. One should consult Matthew and Luke for descriptions of the specific temptations that occurred. Yet there are some distinctive features in Mark's account. For example, the verb "impelled" is the most forceful in any of the accounts in describing the Spirit's initiative. Satan did not ambush Jesus in a weak moment, but rather was confronted by our Lord under the Spirit's energetic leading. It is as though God were saying to Satan, "Here He is. Try your worst. You will find no flaw in Him."

The setting for the temptation is placed in the wilderness. John's preaching and baptizing was also said to be in the wilderness (v. 4), but the temptation narrative implies a somewhat different location. Probably the contrast is between the Jordan River and a more desolate, rugged area. It seems most likely a reference to the wilderness of Judea, a wild and mountainous region between the Judean hills and the Jordan Valley.

Mark also notes that the temptation occurred in the wilderness where the wild beasts were. It was a region devoid of human habitation and open to hostile attacks from wild animals, along with physical deprivation due to the inhospitable conditions. Thus Christ was solely dependent upon His Father, the Spirit, and angelic ministration for survival during these forty days.

## Truths to Remember

• The Gospels are not carbon copies of one another. Each one has its distinctive features and deserves to be studied for its individual contribution.

Fig. 1. Wilderness of Judea, site of Christ's temptations. Wadi Qilt from left foreground diagonally to top center. The Jordan Valley and Jericho are in the distance.

• Because Mark's Gospel is based upon the preaching of the apostle Peter, it has as much claim to apostolic authority as do the gospels of Matthew and John. (Luke was likewise the close associate of the apostle Paul, and thus his Gospel was also readily accepted by the church from the beginning.)

# Part I

## The Ministry in Galilee
### Mark 1:14–9:50

# 2

# PREACHING AND TEACHING IN GALILEE
## Mark 1:14–2:17

After the opening events of John the Baptist's preaching, his baptism of Jesus, and Satan's subsequent temptation of Christ in the wilderness, Mark's account moves immediately into Christ's great Galilean ministry. No note is taken of the fact that there was a period of ministry in Judea and Samaria prior to this (see John 1–4). This procedure is strikingly similar to the way Peter explained the ministry of Christ in his sermon to Cornelius: "You know what has happened throughout Judea, beginning in Galilee after the baptism that John preached—how God anointed Jesus of Nazareth with the Holy Spirit and power, and how he went around doing good and healing all who were under the power of the devil, because God was with him" (Acts 10:37–38 NIV). It seems clear that Mark has followed the pattern of Peter's preaching, just as the earliest Christian writers asserted.[1]

The beginnings of Christ's public ministry in Galilee consisted of the calling of certain ones to be with Him on a permanent basis, His performing of miracles, and the teaching of multitudes at various places around the lake.

[1]See Chapter 1, "Authorship of the Gospel," 2.

## Call of Four Disciples by the Sea, 1:14–20

This event had been preceded by the enlisting of Jesus' first followers—probably John, Andrew, Simon Peter, Philip, and Nathanael (John 1:35–51), the miracle of changing water into wine at Cana in Galilee (John 2:1–11), a visit to Jerusalem for Passover (John 2:13–22), the interview with Nicodemus (John 3:1–21), and the return to Galilee through Samaria where Jesus spoke with the Samaritan woman and taught many in Sychar (John 4:1–42).

One of the reasons why Jesus left Judea was the arrest of John the Baptist. The imprisonment of the one who was pointing the nation to Jesus as the Messiah meant that the focus of hostility would now be concentrated against Jesus. He would not be able to accomplish His preaching and teaching ministry if the authorities were continually hounding Him and intimidating His followers. Humanly speaking, this was why Jesus focused the major portion of His ministry in Galilee, rather than Judea.

As Jesus preached, He announced that the kingdom that had been promised to Israel had come near. This message was a continuation of what John had been preaching. Such prophecies as Daniel's "seventy weeks" (Dan. 9:24–29) were ready for fulfillment. Christ the King had come. This kingdom would not be just a new political regime, however. Entrance to it demanded a spiritual change. Thus, Jesus called upon men to respond to the good news by repentance and faith. Mark's mention of Christ's proclaiming that "the kingdom of God" was at hand is cited by Matthew in the parallel passage as "the kingdom of heaven." This seems to be a clear indication that the two expressions are interchangeable in the Gospels.

As Jesus encountered Simon and Andrew at the Sea of Galilee, we must remember that He had met these men some months previously in Judea (see John 1:41). At that time they had come to an initial faith. Now in this encounter by the sea, they were asked to commit themselves to Him as permanent disciples.

Mark says nothing about the miraculous catch of fish that preceded the call (Luke 5:1–11). The accounts can be harmonized in the following fashion: The four men were engaged in casting and mending nets when Christ first approached. Jesus spoke to the crowds on shore and then made use of a boat as a platform. Afterward, He produced the miraculous catch. Upon returning to shore, as James and John were mending the broken net, Jesus called the four, two at a time, to follow Him.[2] His invitation revealed that He wished to use them in reaching others.

Verse 18 notes the prompt response of the brothers Simon (Peter) and Andrew to follow Jesus. The passing months since their first meeting with Jesus had deepened their conviction, and they decided to join Him permanently. No less responsive were two other brothers, James and John. Their father, Zebedee, offered no objection, and presumably continued his business with the hired servants (vv. 19–20).

---

[2]Some harmonists do not regard the Lukan account as referring to the same event but to a similar one some time later. See R. L. Thomas and S. N. Gundry, *A Harmony of the Gospels* (Chicago: Moody Press, 1978), 52. Robertson, however, favors viewing the three accounts as one event. See A. T. Robertson, *A Harmony of the Gospels for Students of the Life of Christ* (New York: Harper & Brothers, 1950), 33.

## Casting Out a Demon in Capernaum, 1:21–28

Capernaum, a city on the northwest shore of Galilee, served as a sort of headquarters for Jesus during His ministry. Synagogues frequently used guest speakers, and this provided Jesus with an advantageous place from which to get His message to the people. His hearers were astonished by His authoritative manner, which was far different from the rabbis (vv. 22, 27) who, on the contrary, continually appealed to tradition or to the pronouncements of illustrious rabbis from the past. But Jesus came from God with a message that He was empowered to deliver in His own right.

On this occasion the service was interrupted by a man under the control of a demonic spirit. Although the demon immediately recognized the deity of Christ, our Lord did not desire this testimony from an obviously evil source, for it would not be wholesome in its ultimate effects. With a word of command, He ordered the demon to leave the man. As he left his victim, the demon produced a convulsion, but Luke reports that no injury resulted (Luke 4:35). The mixture of the plural personal pronouns "we" and "us" with the singular "I" in the demonic response to Jesus seems to indicate the frequent confusing of the voice of the victim with the persona of the demon or demons. Perhaps the demon controlling the man used "we" because he was speaking for the rest of the demon fraternity who recognized the threat Jesus posed to them.[3]

This synagogue service brought widespread fame to Jesus, both because of the authority He displayed in His teaching and because of His power in the supernatural realm.

---

[3]France, R. T., *The Gospel of Mark* in *The New International Greek Commentary* (Grand Rapids: Eerdmans, 2002), 103.

24

Fig. 2. Excavation of an octagonal church at Capernaum built over Peter's presumed house. A modern shrine has recently been built over this structure.

## Healing of Peter's Mother-in-Law and Others, 1:29–34

Following the synagogue service Jesus entered the home of Peter and Andrew, probably for the Sabbath meal. Remains of an apparent house-church have been found beneath an octagonal church in Capernaum, and the possibility exists that this could have been the house of Peter that is mentioned in this incident. It is very likely that Peter's house would have been one of the first meeting places in that town, and that in later centuries a church building would have been erected over it.[4]

[4]Loffreda, Stanislao. *Recovering Capharnaum* (Jerusalem: Edizioni Custodia Terra Santa, 1985).

At the same house, Peter's mother-in-law was ill. When Jesus was appealed to for aid, He immediately restored her to full health. In spite of the fever, which often produces lingering weakness, her cure was complete with no convalescence necessary. At once she was able to perform her tasks as hostess.

This was an extremely busy day in Christ's ministry. It began with teaching and an exorcism in the synagogue, followed by a healing in Peter's home at meal time. Later that day when evening came, word of Jesus' presence had spread, and soon a tremendous crowd had gathered at the door bringing with them all kinds of afflicted folk. As part of Christ's ministry, to authenticate His authority as one sent from God, He healed all who came to Him. (The Epistles, however, reveal that Christians are not promised freedom from all ills during this age when Christ is absent. See 2 Cor. 12:7–10, Phil. 2:25–27, 2 Tim. 4:20.)

## First Tour of Galilee, 1:35–39

Jesus may have been lodging at Peter's home. The next morning before the others were up, Jesus slipped away to pray, away from the crowds that were sure to come. As Son of Man and as the perfect Servant of Jehovah, our Lord submitted Himself to the Father's leading for all things. Thus, He prayed before starting on a new preaching mission. If He felt the need for prayer, how much more should we!

Eventually, Peter and the others tracked Him down, and informed Him that already the crowds were beginning to congregate, just as they had the day before. Jesus, however, proposed a tour of the neighboring villages, rather than spending all His time in Capernaum. The conviction that this was what He should do may have come or been deepened by the time spent in solitary prayer. This plan was followed, and He undertook the first of three tours of Galilee.

## Healing of a Leper, 1:40–45

Probably while Jesus was on the tour described above, a leper appealed to Him for help. Leprosy was a loathsome disease that in its worst form was incurable. It resulted in ceremonial uncleanness and demanded complete separation from most social contacts. Jesus must have been in the countryside, not in a village, for this leper to have contacted Him. The man seems to have had some doubt about Christ's willingness to cleanse him, although not about His ability. Mark is the only Gospel that tells us that on this occasion Jesus was moved with compassion. He was truly sympathetic to human suffering, and it moved Him to action. When Jesus touched the leper to heal him, did this contact render Jesus ceremonially unclean? One can argue endlessly about whether the leprosy was gone just before He touched him, or afterward. The wise comment of R. T. France seems appropriate: "The touch which should have made Jesus unclean in fact worked in the opposite direction."[5]

After the miracle Jesus sent the man to the priest that he might be pronounced officially cured. This was a regulation of the Mosaic Law (Lev. 14:1). Because of official opposition to Jesus, it would have been better if the priests could have examined the man without any prejudice. If they knew that Jesus had been involved, they might have refused clearance to the man. Thus Jesus cautioned him to silence. The man, however, just could not keep silent. Although what he did was

[5]France, op. cit., 118.

disobedience, it was not malicious, and was psychologically understandable.

## Healing of a Paralytic in Capernaum, 2:1–12

### The Scene at Capernaum, vv. 1–4

The first tour of Galilee was now over, and Jesus had returned to His headquarters in the lakeside city of Capernaum, to which He had moved from Nazareth (Matt. 4:13–16). The mention of "at home" (Greek: "in the house") can be understood as a reference to the house of Peter in the previous context (Mark 1:29), or more likely to the house in which Jesus had settled (note the translation of NASB "He was at home," and NIV "He had come home").

During this stage of Christ's ministry His popularity was very great. On this occasion the house was teeming with people, and the doorway was completely blocked. What attracted the crowds was the incomparable preaching of Jesus. The word that He proclaimed was the chief element of His ministry and was the revelation from God that salvation was being offered to men by the gift of God's Son (v. 2).

In the midst of this busy scene there appeared four men carrying a fifth upon a stretcher-like pallet. The victim was so paralyzed that he could not walk. When they could not gain access to Jesus by the door, they tried a bold and dramatic scheme. Palestinian homes usually had flat roofs that were reached by an outside stairway. The four men carried the paralytic up the stairs, uncovered the tiles that formed the roof, and lowered the stretcher between the joists to the very presence of Jesus. This did no permanent damage to the house and was a most imaginative solution to the problem.

### Jesus' Response to Faith, v. 5

The statement about their faith must refer to the faith of all five—the bearers and the sufferer—for the subsequent pronouncement of forgiveness could come only if the sufferer exercised faith in Christ. Thus, it was not merely the friends who brought the man to Jesus who had faith, but also the invalid, or else he would not have consented to being brought.

"Your sins are forgiven." This announcement by Jesus indicates that the man must have had faith beyond just believing that a miracle was possible. His faith in Christ must have extended to an acceptance of Jesus Himself (as much of Him as the man knew at the time), and thus his sins could be forgiven on the basis of it.

### An Objection Raised by Scribes, vv. 6–7

The men who objected were the professional teachers and interpreters of the Mosaic Law. They were sitting in Jesus' presence and objected to His words. They must have come early to be able to take in all that went on, rather than watch from the edge of the crowd. Luke's Gospel (5:17) indicates that these were not local people but were probably officials from Jerusalem. Their hostility to Christ is seen in their reasoning about Him. Although this was still early in Christ's ministry, the religious leaders of the nation had already shown their official antagonism to Jesus (John 2:14–16). One of the reasons Jesus had left Judea and returned to Galilee was the growing attention that the hostile Pharisees were paying to His rising popularity (John 4:1–3).

As they viewed the events, the Pharisees were first amazed, and then they evaluated what had happened. When they said that God alone has the prerogative to forgive sins, they were correct. On their assumption that Jesus was a mere man, they could not avoid the conclusion that He blasphemed, for forgiveness of sins is not a divine power that God shares with others. The error of the scribes was their refusal to entertain the idea that Jesus was more than a mere man. This charge of blasphemy was eventually the one that the Jews used to condemn Jesus and deliver Him to the Romans for crucifixion.

**Jesus' Explanation Shows His Omniscience, vv. 8–11**

He knew without being told what their thoughts were (v. 8). This fact alone should have deeply impressed these scribes, if they had been disposed to heed it.

Jesus asked which was easier: to pronounce forgiveness or to heal the paralytic. As far as merely saying the words was concerned, one statement was as simple to utter as the other. And from God's standpoint, they were equally easy for Him to perform. However, from the human standpoint, it might be understood that it is easier to say that sins are forgiven, because the results cannot be checked, whereas it is harder to proclaim a healing, because the result (or lack of it) is immediately visible. Yet from another standpoint, the forgiveness of sins is incomparably harder, for prophets could often heal, but only God can absolve a man's sin.

Because men have no way of checking immediately on the results of pronouncing forgiveness, Jesus proceeded to heal the man. This was a visible verification which would be difficult to deny. If He could perform the one miracle, they had no basis for denying His power to perform the other. The words "on the earth" indicate that by the incarnation, forgiveness was not restricted to heaven but was available to be dispensed on earth by the Son of God (vv. 10–11).

**Not Gradual, but an Immediate and Public Cure, v. 12**

Everyone present was astonished. When Mark says that "all" were glorifying God, we need not infer that the scribes were included. This is a general statement to which there could be isolated exceptions. In his parallel account Matthew indicated that it was the multitudes of common people who did the glorifying (Matt. 9:8).

## The Call of Levi, 2:13–17

### The Call at Capernaum, vv. 13–14

Jesus was at the Galilee seashore city of Capernaum. Many of the activities in Christ's ministry occurred around this beautiful lake. Mark records that Jesus was teaching the crowds when He came upon Levi, who was at his tax office. Levi is also the name he is given in Luke 5:27, but he is called Matthew in the first Gospel (Matt. 9:9). Capernaum was a border town between the tetrarchies of Antipas and Philip. Taxes could be collected on goods transported in the region, as well as from ships docking at this port city. Levi's designation as a tax collector marks him as a lower official than Zaccheus, who was a "chief tax-gatherer" (Luke 19:2). Levi was one of a number of tax gatherers in the area, as indicated by the guests at his dinner (v. 15), and his departure to follow Jesus did not leave the tax office unmanned.

To the call, "Follow me," Levi responded at once. One wonders whether there had been some prior contact between Levi and Jesus (as there had been between Jesus and the four fishermen before their call to permanent discipleship). Probably Levi had heard Jesus during His public preaching in Galilee and was now ready to devote his life to Him. As he "rose and followed," he was severing his occupational ties.

31

He could not return to his job (as could fishermen), for his place would be filled by another. Yet, it was this complete commitment that Jesus was looking for.

### A Dinner at Levi's Home, v. 15

The converted tax official gave this dinner to mark the momentous occasion of his discipleship.[6] To it he invited many of his former colleagues and unconverted friends. Because tax collectors worked either directly or indirectly for Rome and were often guilty of extortion, they were despised by most Jews and were viewed along with flagrant sinners as ungodly by the religious element of the nation. Jesus was undoubtedly the guest of honor at this gathering. Surely Levi must have had some evangelistic purpose in mind in arranging it. However, Mark also notes that many of these tax-gatherers and other irreligious folk were attracted to Jesus, even apart from Levi's witness.

### Scribes and Pharisees Left Shocked, v. 16

There were some scribes and Pharisees who were shocked that Jesus would associate with these irreligious people. They felt that this indicated a lack of purity on Jesus' part. They failed to recognize that this was not mere socializing. They should have realized that the purpose of the gathering was to present these people with Christ and His message, in hopes that many of them would be won as Levi had been. It is possible to maintain contact with unbelievers without compromising one's testimony.

---

[6]The location of the dinner is made clear by Luke 5:29, and it is also clarified that "his house" refers to the house of Levi, not the home of Jesus.

**Jesus' Explanation, v. 17**

Jesus defended His action by telling the objectors that it is those who are obviously ailing who need the physician. Thus, His preaching to sinners was basic to the accomplishment of His ministry. When He said He did not come to call righteous ones, but sinners, He was not pronouncing the Pharisees righteous but stating that His dealing with sinners was exactly in harmony with His purpose in coming. The self-righteous Pharisees needed to take a closer look at themselves, and recognize that in God's sight "There is none righteous, not even one" (Rom. 3:10; cf. Ps. 14:1–3; 53:1–3).

It may be profitable to consider ways in which Christians can keep the lines of social communication open with unbelievers, in order to provide opportunities for witnessing, and at the same time not compromise purity of life. How can the Christian keep himself separate from sin and sinners, and yet not become a social misfit who is utterly cut off from the very people whom he is spiritually obligated to reach? Jesus Himself gave us an example. He was not a social misfit. He knew how to maintain His testimony without compromise and without being offensive in the most diverse circumstances.

## Truths to Remember

• Jesus, the Son of God, prayed before undertaking the activities of His ministry. Even He who had no sin felt the need for communion with the Father.

• The miracles of Jesus were not just mechanical displays of power but were usually performed in the realm of human suffering to alleviate men's distress. They displayed the compassionate character of the Savior, who continues to exercise this concern (Heb. 2:17, 4:15).

• Christ values faith, and always responds to those who will trust Him.

• Separation from sin should not cause us to lose our opportunities to witness to sinners.

# 3

# MORE MINISTRY IN GALILEE
## Mark 2:18–3:35

Mark presents Jesus as a many-sided person. He could move easily among the rural folk of Galilee. But He was by no means awkward when discoursing with the high officials of His nation. He could preach to a vast audience and hold it spellbound. He could also reach the heart of a single individual in private interview. He could debate His opponents with incomparable skill, or He could explain the deepest spiritual truths with the simplest stories. He was as much at home by the lakeside as He was in the synagogue. Not only did He fit easily into the most diverse situations, but He also had a contribution to make to each one.

For Mark, the writer who was interested in action, this many-sidedness of Jesus was particularly appealing. As Jesus continued His ministry in Galilee, He is described by Mark in a variety of settings. In each one He had a significant contribution to make, and through these contributions, He ministered to the needs of men. Present-day readers should find this fact reassuring.

## Discussion with the Pharisees and Others, 2:18–3:6

### Fasting, 2:18–22

*The Problem, v. 18.* Fasting was a fairly common practice among the Jews. Although the Mosaic Law required only one fast per year (the Day of Atonement),[1] Jews had added four other annual fasts during the Exile,[2] and by the time of Jesus some pious Jews fasted twice weekly (Monday and Thursday).[3] Fasting was often an opportunity for a public display of piety, and Jesus spoke sharply against the ostentatious fasting-for-fasting's-sake in the Sermon on the Mount (Matt. 6:16–18). It is possible that this incident occurred on one of the days when many Jews were fasting. Perhaps Jesus and the disciples had recently come from the feast at Levi's house, while the questioners had been fasting all day. Thus, their question was, "Why do the followers of John the Baptist and many of the followers of the Pharisees practice fasting, while Jesus and His disciples obviously do not?" The questioners are not identified. Since the disciples of Jesus and those of John and the Pharisees are referred to in the third person, we may assume that those who asked the question belonged to neither group.

*The Explanation, vv. 19–20.* Jesus likened His ministry to a wedding. He asked if the participants in a wedding would practice fasting in the presence of the bridegroom. The obvious answer was no. Fasting is most inappropriate in the midst of a wedding. In applying this illustration, Jesus was likening himself to the bridegroom (the same illustration is used of Jesus by John in John 3:29). As long as He was present, it was time to rejoice, not to mourn and fast.

However, things would not always be this way. Christ was going to be taken away from His disciples by violent death. Even though death would be followed by resurrection and ascension, the coming separation would bring great hardship

[1]Lev. 16:29–34.
[2]Zech. 7:5; 8:19.
[3]Luke 18:12.

to His followers. There would be persecution and fasting (both voluntary and involuntary). The New Testament does not legislate any formal fasts for the church. However, there is scriptural indication that fasting was practiced voluntarily by the early church on certain occasions (Acts 13:2). In times of special stress, or in devoting oneself without interruption to prayer or Bible study, fasting can be an aid. But it must not be legislated, or engaged in merely to display one's piety.

*Two Analogies, vv. 21–22.* A good story often lodges in the memory much better than an unadorned explanation. In this passage, Jesus illustrated the truth of what He had said with two simple word pictures. No one, He said, sews a patch of unshrunken cloth upon an old, worn-out garment, because as soon as the garment with the new patch is washed, the patch will shrink and will tear away the fragile edges of the older garment. The teaching was obvious, so Jesus did not need to spell out the application. His ministry was not a mere patch upon Judaism. It was something new which justified new methods.

The second word picture illustrates the same principle. In Jesus' day liquids were frequently stored or carried in containers made of goat skins. The hide was removed from the animal in one piece, and the neck and leg holes were sewn shut. When new wine was stored in a wineskin, the "bottle" would stretch as the wine fermented. No one, however, would put new wine into an old wineskin, for as it fermented it would put pressure on the wineskin and an old one would have no further elasticity. It would almost certainly split, thus spilling the wine and rendering the wineskin useless. So Christ's teaching, while not unrelated to Old Testament revelation, brought something new.

Consequently, it demanded a different method from John's, or the notions of the Pharisees.

### The Sabbath, 2:23–28

*The Problem, vv. 23–24.* There is no indication that this event followed immediately after the previous incident in Mark. Most likely it occurred in Galilee after a visit to Jerusalem which only John's Gospel records (John 5). One Sabbath day Jesus and His disciples were walking in the country. Apparently they had left the regular path and were walking through someone's grain field. This, of course, was common practice and would raise no questions. During their walk the disciples plucked some handfuls of grain[4] and were eating them as they went. This practice was specifically mentioned and approved in the Mosaic Law, provided that one did not use a sickle (Deut. 23:25).

Some Pharisees must have been observing. Perhaps there was a large crowd accompanying Jesus, as was often the case. What they objected to was not plucking the grain, but it was being done on the Sabbath. Thus they charged the disciples, and by implication Jesus, with Sabbath violation. According to some strict interpreters among them, plucking the grain was a form of reaping, and thus it was work. The Old Testament did not say this in so many words, but some felt they were applying the principle of the fourth commandment.

*Historical Illustrations, vv. 25–26.* Before Jesus gave His own explanation of the proper use of the Sabbath, He cited an illustration from the Old Testament. When He asked, "Have

---

[4]This was probably wheat or barley, but not, as translated by KJV, "ears of corn" for this crop was unknown in Palestine.

you never read?" He was expecting an affirmative answer. We might paraphrase it this way: "You have certainly read the case of David, haven't you?" He knew these Pharisees were well-versed in the Scripture. However, it often seemed that they paid more attention to rabbinic law than to Scripture.

The passage to which Jesus referred is 1 Samuel 21:1–6. It describes the incident in which David and his band of followers were fleeing from the wrath of King Saul. At this time the Tabernacle was at Nob. David entered the outer court (where any Jew could go) and asked for provisions from the high priest. The only food available was the shewbread, which was for the priests alone. The custom was that twelve fresh loaves were baked each Friday and placed on the table in the holy place at the start of the Sabbath. The old bread was removed at the same time and deposited at the entry of the sanctuary, where incoming and outgoing priests could eat it. Yet, because of the need of David and his men, they partook of it and received no rebuke from God, nor was David ever condemned in later years by Pharisean interpreters.[5]

*The Explanation, vv. 27–28.* Jesus here interpreted the real meaning of the Sabbath commandment. Mark is the only Gospel to record this saying. Jesus explained that God instituted the Sabbath for man's benefit. It was to contribute to his well-being, physical and spiritual. Yet, the Pharisees and rabbis seemed to suggest by their regulations that

---

[5]Compare Christ's statement with the 1 Samuel 21 account and note an apparent discrepancy. Jesus called the priest Abiathar, but he is called Ahimelech in the Old Testament. Actually, Ahimelech was the father of Abiathar. Possible solutions are that both names were borne by the father as well as the son (see 2 Sam. 8:17; 1 Chron. 18:16; 24:3, 6, 31), or both father and son were present when David came to Nob. The father died shortly thereafter, and Abiathar became high priest. He may have been the one who recorded the facts here cited.

the Sabbath was an institution to which men must rigidly conform. But man was not created for the purpose of keeping Sabbath laws. On the contrary, the Sabbath was established to minister to man's need. Therefore, at those times when man's welfare demanded it, the Sabbath laws could be set aside.

Using His favorite title for Himself, "the Son of Man," Jesus stated that just as David the future king could set aside a ceremonial regulation because of a human need, so also Jesus, the God-Man and David's prophesied heir, was Lord of the Sabbath and could use the Sabbath for the blessing of men.

### Healing on the Sabbath, 3:1–6

The healing of the man with the withered hand clearly took place in Galilee (see v. 7). The location of the synagogue is not stated, but it may well have been the synagogue at Capernaum, where Jesus often appeared while using that city as His headquarters.

The man with the withered hand is almost a passive character in this episode. He does not approach Jesus, but rather Jesus confronts him. Those who were "watching Him" were looking at the situation with suspicious and hostile intent, as verse 6 makes clear. If we are correct in surmising that Jesus had just returned from Jerusalem where the charge of Sabbath-breaking was leveled against Him, that would explain Mark's inclusion of this episode. The healing is not the focus of the narrative, but the issue of whether Jesus violated the Sabbath regulations.

Jesus invited the man to stand up in full view of the congregation. This would make the man's condition clear to everyone, and the miracle would be visible to all. Jesus obviously knew what the hostile stares of some indicated.

Fig. 3. Synagogue at Capernaum, dating from the 4th century A.D.
This synagogue was built over an earlier one from the time of
Christ.

In view of the Sabbath controversies He had encountered
in Jerusalem, He understood full well what He was doing.
Then He asked the question, "Is it lawful to do good or to do
evil?" The opponents would hardly answer by the latter; only
the first alternative would be proper. The second part of the
question, "To save a life or to kill?" went to the heart of the
problem with these evil men. This seems to be an instance of
Christ's knowing their thoughts, for in a few minutes these
critics would begin plotting the death of Jesus (v. 6).

Christ looked at these devious critics with anger. This
is the term usually translated as "wrath." It reflects His
continuing antipathy toward sin and its effects in this world.
With Christ, His anger is always righteous. In this instance,
the anger was directed against the unrelenting rebellion in
the hearts of those Pharisees present.

The miracle is described in the simplest of terms. No means were used, not a touch from Jesus, nor even a command for the healing. He merely asked the man to stretch out his hand, and it was restored. The emphasis is clearly not on the miracle, but upon the Sabbath controversy.

The Pharisees are here associated with the Herodians. The latter were not a religious or even a political party, but were supporters of the Herods who wielded political power from Rome. In this instance they would have been supporters of Herod Antipas, ruler of Galilee at this time. Both groups were joined in their hatred of Jesus, who posed a threat to the status quo.

## More Teaching and Healing by the Sea, 3:7–12

In this passage, Jesus gets into a boat and goes out on the Galilean sea to address the crowd on the shore. Some have questioned whether this incident follows immediately in the context of the previous paragraph, but the fact that the parallel account in Matthew 12:15 is preceded by the same incident as Mark records, lends weight to the view that this narrative is in chronological order. Certainly the presence of great crowds, including many hostile listeners from Jerusalem, fits the context well.

The size of the growing crowds caused Jesus to withdraw (from the confines of the synagogue?) to the waterfront. This action did not reduce the number of onlookers, but merely gave them more room to congregate. People were present from all regions of the country, as well as neighboring territories. Mention is made of Galilee, Judea, and Jerusalem, the latter being distinguished from Judea because of its special importance. Idumea was the territory to the south in the Negev.[6] The area beyond the Jordan included Perea and Decapolis, and the vicinity of Tyre and Sidon was the territory of Phoenicia. Mark wants his readers to recognize the growing popularity and influence Jesus was having in the nation.

Only in Mark do readers learn that Jesus had a small boat available to Him for His ministry. Apparently some of His disciples, even though they had left their fishing business to follow Jesus, still had access to a boat, which He used from time to time. It would enable Him to use it as a platform, to escape the crush of the crowds on the shore, and perhaps also to make it possible for Him to move back and forth before the crowds on the shore as He spoke. This need was made evident because some who were seeking healing were actually falling on Him to be healed by His touch (v. 10).

Another group that followed Jesus for His ministration were those possessed by evil spirits. These are clearly distinguished from the former group of persons who needed healing from illnesses. The demon-possessed persons prostrated themselves before Jesus, saying, "You are the Son of God." It was the unvarying practice of demons to indicate precisely the identity of Jesus when they confronted Him. Jesus, however, did not desire such impure testimony, for this would aid the blasphemous charge that He was in league with demons. He preferred to let men know His identity as a result of their personal observation of Him.

---

[6]The name comes from Edom in the Old Testament. After the fall of Jerusalem in 587 B.C., the Edomites migrated into Israel, particularly in the South, and their territory became known as Idumea. They were conquered during the Maccabean Wars and placed under a governor, Antipater, who became the grandfather of Herod the Great. This is the only mention of Idumea in the New Testament.

# Selection of the Twelve, 3:13–19

This incident seems to have followed shortly after the large crowds forced Christ's withdrawal from Capernaum. Mark says He went up to "the mountain." The fact that the mountain is not further identified suggests that it was a well-known and often-used retreat by Jesus and the disciples. Suggestions vary as to its location, but it is most commonly thought to be a hillside in Galilee, probably not far from Capernaum.[7]

As Jesus withdrew to this secluded mountain, He summoned certain ones to go with Him. It appears likely that only those whom He would select as the Twelve were with Him at this time. He appointed them for the special privilege of being with Him regularly and learning from Him. He also would send them out to preach His message as His duly qualified representatives, and He gave them authority to cast out demons.[8] (The entrance of the God-man into human life may have prompted an increase of demonic activity, which caused Jesus to include this provision. God's power would conquer the demons, but the Twelve were authorized to invoke that power.)

Mark's listing of the Twelve is one of four such lists in the New Testament.[9] They are not in the same order, but all list the same persons. Peter is at the head of each list, and if one divides the lists into groups of four, the same four persons appear in each group, with Philip heading the second group,

[7]The traditional identification has been the Horns of Hattin, west of the Sea of Galilee along the Arbell Pass, although no real evidence supports this view.

[8]The phrase "whom He named apostles" is omitted by NASB but is included in the KJV and in the NIV as "designating them apostles." The documentary evidence is mixed but seems too strong to warrant the omission of these words. If they did not appear originally, they were probably imported from Luke 6:13 by a later scribe.

[9]The others are Matt. 10:2–4, Luke 6:14–16, and Acts 1:13.

and James of Alphaeus heading the third group. Mark's Gospel is the only one to mention Jesus' nicknaming of James and John as "sons of thunder." Perhaps this referred to their fiery zeal (Mark. 9:38; Luke. 9:54). The name "Thaddeus" in Mark and Matthew seems to be the same as "Judas the son of James" in Luke and Acts.

At this point in New Testament history Jesus gave the extended Sermon on the Mount to the great crowd who had joined Him (Matt. 5–7). Mark, however, did not include this address in his Gospel, perhaps because he was aware that Matthew's Gospel was already in circulation and had included more discourse material. Of course, this assumes that Mark's Gospel did not originate as the earliest one. For whatever reason, Mark's purpose was to convey more of the activity of Jesus, rather than His extended discourse.

## Accusation by the Pharisees, 3:20–35

When Jesus "came home"[10] to Capernaum, His head-quarters during most of His ministry, the crowds were so insistent to hear Him that He and his disciples could hardly find opportunity to eat. Eventually "His own people"[11] came in order to take charge of the situation. Although not all agree, it is likely the reference is to the family of Jesus, who are mentioned in verses 31–35. The exceedingly strenuous life of Jesus and the opposition He had aroused among the officials had deeply alarmed his family. They felt He needed a rest because (they thought) He was not thinking clearly.

[10]From NASB. The Greek text reads literally "into a house," but the meaning "at home" occurs frequently. Bauer, Arndt, and Gingrich, *A Greek-English Lexicon of the New Testament* (Chicago: University of Chicago Press, 1979), 560.

[11]From NASB. Greek text: *hoi par' autou*. The phrase is difficult in this context, although it seems to mean "those who are associated with Him" in some way. It can hardly refer to the disciples, who are referred to separately in this context. The most common understanding is as a reference to friends or even kinsmen.

Mark inserts into this narrative about Jesus' family a description of one of the chief aggravations at this time. Scribes "came down from Jerusalem"[12] and began accusing Jesus of being in league with Satan. "Beelezebul" here is called the ruler of the demons and is clearly equated with Satan (cf. vv. 23, 26). This explains why Jesus always rebuked the demons who tried to give testimony to His identity. He knew that sort of testimony was subject to misinterpretation.

These assertions were apparently made by the scribes behind Jesus' back, but He knew what they were thinking and so summoned them and refuted their accusations with a series of analogies. If their accusation was true, then Satan would be acting in contradiction to himself, and that would make no sense. If one part of a kingdom fights against another part of that same kingdom, the collapse of the whole is certain unless the rift is stopped. That principle is true even in a much smaller household: if its diverse elements are working against each other, that household is headed for dissolution. Thus if the explanation of Jesus' actions is really the work of Satan, then Satan would be working against himself and his destruction would be inevitable.

Jesus then explained His mission with the story of a robber attempting to plunder a strong man's home. He could be successful only by overpowering the strong man. In this story Satan is the strong man who has control of these poor victims whom Jesus had helped. The fact that Jesus could cast out the demons was proof that He had overpowered Satan, not that He was cooperating with him.

---

[12]Although Jerusalem is south of Galilee, one was always described as going up to the city when approaching it and going down from it when leaving, regardless of compass direction. Jerusalem is on a mountain ridge with an elevation of 2,400+ feet above sea level, whereas Capernaum on the shore of the Sea of Galilee is more than 600 feet below sea level.

Jesus then enlarged his explanation to these scribes by warning them and all the other listeners that failure to recognize who Jesus was and what his Spirit-led ministry was offering to mankind was the most serious of offenses. In fact, there is one blasphemy which God will not forgive. This is the so-called unpardonable sin or the sin against the Holy Ghost, which has been variously interpreted. Some restrict it to this context and explain it as attributing Christ's works on earth to an evil spirit, rather than to the Holy Spirit. Thus it is a sin that could be committed only during the earthly ministry of Christ.

Others, however, note that the New Testament mentions a sin that cannot receive forgiveness, and this was stated to the church long after the Ascension (Heb. 6:4–6; 10:26–31). It seems best to this interpreter to understand the "unpardonable sin" in the following way: because the Bible assures us that "the blood of Jesus His Son cleanses us from *all* sin" (1 John. 1:7), the only conceivable sin that is unforgivable is the final rejection of Christ, who is God's perfect and only provision for us. There is no Plan B. Of course, many have rejected Christ's offer of salvation and later have turned in faith to Him and received forgiveness and salvation. But if one rejects with *finality* that free offer of God's grace in Christ, which the Holy Spirit is bringing before mankind today, then that person is left with the burden of his or her sins for all eternity. The scribes of Jesus' day were rejecting His spirit-led ministry by attributing His work to demonic power.

Verse 31 resumes the narrative from verse 21, and may further identify who "His own people" were. Mark interrupts the narrative at that point to explain the Pharisees' accusation. Such charges against Him, in addition to the strenuous days He was putting in with the crowds, prompted His family to make contact. Even on this occasion the crowds were so great that the family had to send word into the house that they were there to see Him. Mary was there with the brothers[13] of Jesus. Presumably the sisters would have been married with homes of their own, and thus were not present.

Jesus startled His hearers by asking, "Who are My mother and My brothers?" He was preparing them for the idea that the closest relationship to Him, and the most vital one, is not physical. Looking at those seated around Him, who were probably the Twelve and other firm disciples, He indicated that they were in some sense His kinsmen. This relationship is then defined as "Whoever does the will of God" (v. 35).

Doing the will of God, which essentially involves trusting in Christ (John 6:29) produces the closest relationship to Him, a spiritual one. This statement was no disrespect to his physical family, for eventually they too shared this higher relationship with Him.

## Truths to Remember

• It is easy to turn a helpful religious practice into a legalistic code or a burdensome ritual and lose the meaning of the practice. Fasting and keeping the Sabbath are two clear examples.

• Christ does not need testimony from evil sources to support His cause.

• The first responsibility of the Twelve was to learn from Jesus.

---

[13]These would seem to be the younger half-brothers of Jesus, born to Joseph and Mary after Jesus' birth. There are other views, but they are in all likelihood attempts to protect the idea of the perpetual virginity of Mary.

# 4

# A SERIES OF PARABLES ABOUT THE KINGDOM
## Mark 4:1–34

A distinctive feature of Jesus' teaching was His use of parables to convey truth. He was not the originator of this literary form; many others had used it before, but He was surely its master. No one else was able to take so many and such a variety of simple stories and use them to convey deep spiritual truths.

Parables, as used in the New Testament, were stories drawn from life in order to illustrate some spiritual truth. They seem usually, if not always, to be fictitious, although there was nothing unreal in the stories; that is, when Jesus talked about a sower going forth to sow, He did not necessarily have a certain farmer in mind. But the story was true to life, for it could have happened to any sower. This differs from fables such as Aesop's, in which animals talk and all sorts of unreal actions take place.

Jesus used parables to illustrate the truth He was teaching. A good story will stay in the memory long after the bare truth might be forgotten. On some occasions, however, Jesus seemed to have an additional purpose in view. Rather than giving out His deepest truths to the scoffers who had no intention of believing, He sometimes couched them in parables. If a man had sufficient desire to know, he could study them and learn their meaning. But if not, at least he could not disparage all the precious truths of

God's revelation. This was in harmony with the principle that Jesus taught: "Do not throw your pearls before swine" (Matt. 7:6).

Parables are not the simplest portions of Scripture to interpret. Whenever one's thinking moves from the symbolic (parable) to the literal (interpretation), there is opportunity for wrong meaning to be injected. Several principles can help the interpreter. It is important to consider the setting in which the parable is given—particularly the audience and the subject being discussed. Next, one should find the main point being illustrated. Details of the story should be explained in connection with the main point. From the example of Jesus, who interpreted some of His parables for us, it is clear that we must not necessarily attach some specific meaning to every detail in the parable, for in some instances Jesus Himself did not. Some details were included to give form to the story. Much fanciful interpretation has arisen at this point. Finally, we should beware of basing doctrinal teaching solely on the details of a parable. It is never safe to argue from the unclear to the clear. Therefore, the teaching of parables should be checked against other, non-symbolic portions of Scripture.

## The Parable of the Sower, 4:1–20

### The Parable, 4:1–9

This parable was actually the first of a series that Jesus gave on one day. Matthew 13 gives more of the parables of this series than the other Gospels. Mark, however, includes one parable that the others do not mention—the Seed Growing by Itself (vv. 26–29). When Jesus told the parable of the sower, He resumed His practice of teaching along the shore of the Sea of Galilee. He described a Palestinian farmer who went out to plant his field. The Scripture says "the sower" (v. 3). Grammarians call this the generic use of the article, referring to this sower who would be typical of all Palestinian sowers. In those days seed was scattered by hand over a relatively small plot of ground.

According to this story, some of the farmer's seed fell on the hard surface of the packed earth where men walked. In a typical Palestinian unfenced field, a path would meander through the field or along the edge, and some of the seed would naturally fall on its surface. Because this seed did not penetrate the soil, the birds soon spotted it and ate it.

Part of the seed fell on rocky ground. This does not refer to ground with many stones in it but to a rocky ledge covered with a thin layer of soil. Because of the rock beneath, the warmth from the sun would radiate back from the rock and thus the soil would warm more quickly and cause rapid germination. However, the hot sun would swiftly cause the young plant to be scorched. And because the root system of the plant would be impeded by the rock, there was no way for it to obtain moisture. Such a plant would inevitably wither away.

Another portion of the seed fell among thorns. Of course, no one would deliberately sow seeds in a briar patch. Therefore, this must have been bare ground in which thorn seeds already lay. When both types of seeds sprouted, the thorns took over.

Fortunately for the sower, some of his seed fell into soil unhampered by any of those conditions. This was the one productive situation and the yield, while great, was not uncommon in Palestine.

The solemn words, "He who has ears to hear, let him

hear" (v. 9), suggest not only the need to heed Christ's instructions but also that there is a deeper meaning to the parable than lies on the surface. Not all had ears attuned to that message.

Fig. 4. Sower's Cove on northwest shore of the Sea of Galilee, a likely spot for Jesus to have given the parable of the sower and other parables.

### The Explanation, 4:10–20

When it was possible to speak to Jesus somewhat privately, without the hordes of people milling around, a group of disciples, including the Twelve, asked Him about the parables. They realized that this parabolic series was different from mere illustrations.

One should compare the parallel accounts in Matthew 13:11–17 and Luke 8:10 as an aid in understanding this difficult passage. In His explanation Jesus clearly distinguished two kinds of people. One group He called "you," which was comprised of believers who already had been initiated into the realm of God's revealed truth.

They had acquired some spiritual insight and were able to receive more. Because they possessed some knowledge of the kingdom of God ("mystery" [v. 11] in Scripture refers to truth revealed by God that was formerly hidden), they had a basis for interpreting the parables and thus could convey additional truth. He called the other group "them who are outside" (v. 11). These were unbelievers—ones who had bypassed the elements of spiritual knowledge and hence had no capacity to receive advanced truth. It was because of their presence in His audience that He couched His words in parables that day.

Verse 12 is a quotation from Isaiah 6:9–10, which states that God sometimes sends spiritual blindness upon those who have hardened their hearts. We must remember that the unbelievers mentioned here were not uninformed. Rather, they had rejected the message and steeled their hearts against God's truth. These were hardened, determined unbelievers, some of whom had already accused Jesus of being in league with Satan (Mark 3:19–30, Matt. 12:22–37). Since Jesus knew their hearts, He withheld the bare truths from those who were determined to reject them. But those who had spiritual interest could be stimulated by the parables to search out their meaning and come to the truth.

Jesus then explained this parable in detail. Unless the disciples understood the principles of interpreting this first one, they would not be able to interpret the remaining parables in the series.

*The Seed by the Wayside, vv. 14–15.* The seed is defined as the Word of God in Luke 8:11, and the sower, while not interpreted in this parable, pictures Christ (Matt. 13:37) and those who represent Him. The seed sown on the hardened path, which could not penetrate the soil, represents the hardened hearer of the Word who refuses to let God's message of salvation enter his heart. He is the unresponsive hearer whom Satan by his agents (the birds in the parable) is able to deprive of his temporary contact with God's truth. There are many who hear God's Word, but through doubts, negligence, or a thousand other means produced by Satan do not let God's Word become active in their lives.

*The Seed on Stony Ground, vv. 16–17.* This describes those who make an immediate response but whose understanding is shallow. "Joy" suggests that these hearers are emotional, but not necessarily stable. Just as a plant growing on a rock ledge cannot root deeply, so these hearers are momentarily swayed by the excitement of the message, but they do not take permanent root. When affliction or persecution comes (and it is possible in every life), such hearers will not be willing to endure these hardships, for they have not been truly converted.

*The Seed among Thorns, vv. 18–19.* Once again the difference in response is traced not to the seed, but to the soil conditions. This soil is preoccupied with the seeds of thorns. Whatever response there was initially to the preaching of the Word was soon choked out by earthly interests and desire for wealth. The first attraction to God's Word is prevented from coming full circle, because the concerns of this present age loom too large. In these three types of hearers, the response is shown to be absent or aborted. The problem was not with the seed, for it was the same in each case. The difficulty lay in the condition present in the soil. It was hard and unresponsive, open but shallow, or preoccupied with powerful rivals.

Thus, Jesus taught that when His Word is proclaimed, we can expect a variety of responses. When not all receive it, we must not become discouraged with the seed, for God's Word is still able to bring new birth. The fault lies in the sinful condition of human hearts.

*The Seed on Good Ground, v. 20.* This described the only group to be commended. These hearers listen to the Gospel and accept it. Because the Word is the power of God to salvation (Rom. 1:16), it is certain to be effective in every life which receives it. Although there is a difference in the amount of fruitfulness (corresponding to the differences among true Christians), all made some fruitful response, and none is regarded as unsatisfactory.

Christ was the original Sower who proclaimed to men the good news of salvation. Since the Ascension the sowing has continued through His representatives. Everyone who tells another about salvation in Christ is sowing the seed. Lest we be disheartened when the response to our witness is not 100 percent favorable, Jesus gave this parable to show that there is nothing wrong with the seed but that conditions in the soil will cause a variety of responses. It is our task to sow the seed. Some of it will fall on good ground.

## The Parable of the Lamp, 4:21–25

### The Parable, 4:21–23

Jesus told this story to enforce the truth of the Parable of the Sower. He told of a lamp, which in His day was a small clay vessel into which olive oil was poured. A wick was inserted in one opening, and when lighted, it provided illumination for the user. He asked if anyone would bring such a lighted lamp into a room and then put it underneath a bowl (NIV; literally, "peck measure") or beneath a bed. Obviously, such an act would contradict the purpose of procuring the lamp. Common practice would be to place it upon a lampstand so that its light could illuminate the whole room and be used by many. These words were directed particularly to those who had received the Word and had understood it. They were now to dispense it to others, not hide it. The fact that some hearers will not respond is no excuse for us to hide the truth.

Jesus further clarified the point by saying, "For nothing is hidden, except to be revealed." Although man's purpose in hiding things is to conceal them, God has a way of bringing man's hidden things to light. Here, however, Jesus seems to refer to God's purpose in hiding certain truths in parables (vv. 11–12). That purpose was eventually to bring to light what would otherwise be lost if not deposited in parabolic form. "If any man has ears to hear, let him hear." The repetition of this solemn exhortation (v. 9) encourages those with spiritual hearing to use it.

### The Explanation, 4:24–25

In view of the instruction which His believing hearers had received, Jesus urged them to measure up to their new responsibility. Those who heard and received the teaching that Jesus gave them would be blessed with an appropriate increase in understanding God's truth. This spiritual principle continues to operate. When one is receptive to God's Word and the enlightenment which God's Spirit furnishes regarding it, his spiritual capacity becomes greater. Thus, the more he comprehends spiritually, the more he is able to receive.

Sadly enough, the opposite is also true. Those who fail to give attentive hearing to God's Word will eventually lose even that superficial understanding of God's truth they may now have.

## The Parable of the Seed Growing by Itself, 4:26–29

The Parable of the Seed Growing by Itself occurs only in Mark's Gospel. Yet, its symbolism is quite similar to the others given on this one occasion.

Jesus said that the parable depicts something about the kingdom of God. A comparison of all the parables in the series indicates that He was referring to the unusual form which this kingdom would take, beginning with Christ's first coming until He returns to earth to establish His millennial reign. Although the externals of the kingdom are not yet in operation and must await the Second Coming of Christ, God is active today, calling out from the nations believers who will reign with His Son, and these are said to be in the kingdom now (Col. 1:13). The parable, then, describes what the normal growth of the kingdom is like during the present age.

Several of the symbols in this parable are the same as others in the series and are used in the same way. There is a sower, seed, and ground. The ground here is pictured as responsive and thus is the same as the good ground in the Parable of the Sower. It stands for those human hearts in the world which are responsive to the Word of God. The seed symbolizes the Word of God, as in the previous parable, which when sprouted results in born-again believers. The man who sows the seed seems to picture the representatives of Christ, rather than Christ Himself (since the man doesn't know how the seed grows up, but Christ certainly does). Thus, the parable was an explanation to Christ's followers of how His kingdom would develop in the world during this period prior to His return.

### Growth Requires the Planting of the Seed

This is self-evident in the physical realm. As long as the seed remains in the sack, it won't produce any harvest. It must be taken out and committed to the soil. So the Word of God must be planted in human hearts if it is to mature in human lives.

In all the parables of this series the seed is the Word of God. We must not suppose that social reform, nuclear disarmament, or community betterment is the message that must take precedence. Rather, God's message of salvation through faith in Jesus Christ must be proclaimed to men. It is our duty, as those who call Christ our Lord, to serve Him by proclaiming His message.

### Growth Depends on the Power in the Seed

The parable describes the sower as having full confidence in the good seed he planted. Once he had committed it to the ground, he could resume his normal activity without anxiety. He could sleep at night and rise to other tasks in the day without worry. He need not dig up the seed for periodic inspection, for the seed contained within itself the power of germination and growth. No criticism is implied against the sower sleeping at night.

In like manner we must repose full confidence in the Word of God, for it is no ordinary message. We should not suppose our task is to bolster the Scripture with our puny explanations. We must rather declare "Thus says the Lord," and trust it to do the work. Just as the farmer does not need to be able to explain all the processes of growth in order to reap the benefits ("how, he himself does not know"), so we cannot explain how God takes the simple message of salvation and uses it to implant eternal life by His Spirit (John 3:8). The important thing to remember is that God does do it. The Gospel is "the power of God for salvation to every one who believes" (Rom. 1:16).

### Growth Occurs in Stages

We are not to expect an immediate harvest. "First the blade, then the head, then the mature grain in the head" (v. 28). New "plants" in Christ are not immediately mature. But there should be growth. We should not become impatient with the babes in Christ, but neither should we be satisfied if there is no progress toward spiritual maturity. There is also to be growth of the spiritual body as a whole. Each convert brings the full crop that much closer to completion.

### Growth Will Eventually Be Complete

Someday the last person will be gathered in and Christ will harvest His crop. The growth for which He is waiting will be complete, and He will return. This is the truth He taught with this parable — that during His absence He has not abandoned His people but is granting time for the Word to produce its work of growth in their lives.

## The Parable of the Mustard Seed, 4:30–34

The previous parable depicted the normal growth pattern in Christ's kingdom. The Parable of the Mustard Seed pictures an unusual feature of its growth.

## The Seed

The mustard seed was a symbol in Christ's time for that which was very small. It was the smallest of the seeds that might be planted in a garden. Consistent with the other parables in the series, the seed represents the Word of God. Certainly the teaching of Christ seemed insignificant at first when compared to men's usual ideas of a kingdom. It stressed humility rather than physical power. It made no claims to wealth. It involved the death of its king. Yet, this seed grew in a remarkable way. Just as the Palestinian mustard plant becomes very large in comparison to the size of its seed, so the number of Christ's followers grow from a few adherents to more than 3,000 at Pentecost until the Roman Empire adopted Christianity by the fourth century.

## The Unusual Growth

This mustard plant from a small beginning became greater than all the garden herbs. Once full grown, its unusual size reminds us of the vast size of Christendom today. More people are church members today than ever before. But the parable suggests there is something unusual and perhaps even abnormal about all this.

## The Birds in the Branches

Because the plant that grows from the mustard seed becomes so large, many creatures who are not a part of the tree are able to use its protection. "Birds" in this series of parables are symbols of evil (4:4; cf. 4:15). Thus, Jesus taught that while He was gone, the gospel that He gave would attract a following that would greatly multiply, but the enemies of God would invade and take refuge among them. This has occurred in a variety of ways. Today commercial enterprises, humanitarian movements, and even governments identify themselves as "Christian" to further their own ends. Believers are forewarned by the parable to be sure they are part of the true growth of God's plant.

## Truths to Remember

• Our response to God's Word reveals the kind of heart we have.

• When God grants us blessing, He thereby increases our responsibility to bless others.

• Not everything that claims to be "Christian" is necessarily so. It may be a bird in the branches rather than a part of the tree.

# 5

# A SERIES OF MIRACLES
## Mark 4:35–5:43

Jesus' miracles are some of the most outstanding aspects of His career. Yet, He was neither the first man nor the last to employ supernatural power, for certain men in the Old Testament (such as Moses, Elijah, and Elisha) worked miracles; and later the apostles did so also.

It is a common opinion today that the miracles of the Bible are not historically reliable. The idea is prevalent in our scientific and skeptical age that no true miracle is possible. Miracles, however, are not that easily removed from the Bible. They are woven so thoroughly into the fabric of the Gospel records that they cannot be deleted without destroying their portrayal of Christ.

Anyone who is willing to read the Bible and accept it as trustworthy must take the miracles along with the rest. The Christ of the Sermon on the Mount is also the Christ who performed miracles. If it can be believed that what He taught was true (that is, that He was the very Son of God), then one should not stumble at the fact that He also demonstrated some of the works of God in miracles. Nor should it be a surprise to learn that the God who made the world did not thereafter shut Himself out of it. The God who established the order of nature did not obligate Himself to refrain forever from injecting a new element into it. He did this when He sent the flood (Genesis 7). He could and did inject new elements again through miracles.

Although others besides Christ performed miracles, there were certain features about His that were distinctive. His miracles were always accomplished with the greatest ease, whereas the miracles of others were often performed with some difficulty. Compare how easily Christ raised Lazarus (John 11) or the daughter of Jairus (Mark 5) with the experience of Elisha in raising the child of the Shunamite woman (2 Kings 4:34–35).

The miracles of Jesus were all gracious and merciful acts. Often in the Old Testament, miracles were acts of judgment (leprosy inflicted, death imposed, and so on). Furthermore, Jesus was not dependent on any instrument of power outside Himself. Others often needed a rod or a mantle or some other instrument, but Jesus' own will and word were sufficient. His use of clay to anoint the eyes of the blind man (John 9:6–9) was clearly optional, for on another occasion He healed a blind man without using clay (Mark 10:51–52).

It should not be supposed, however, that miracles are always performed by divine power and that every miracle worker must be heeded. In Deuteronomy 13:1–5, Israel was warned that supernatural power can be utilized by Satan as well. Therefore, whenever a miracle was performed and investigation proved it was not a fake, then the people were to test the teachings of the miracle worker to determine the source of his power. If he had used the miracle to lead the people away from the truth God had already revealed, they were to recognize him as a false prophet and deal with him appropriately.

Thus, the Jews of Jesus' day were responsible to test His miracles by His teaching. If He used the miracles to gain a following and then to teach them contrary to revealed truth in the Old Testament, He was to be condemned. On the other hand, if His teaching was in perfect harmony with what God's Word has revealed, they should view the miracles as the divine authentication of His ministry.

In this portion of Mark's Gospel, four miracles depict Christ's authority in various realms. Whether in the realm of nature, the unseen world of evil spirits, serious illness, or even death, Jesus is shown to be the Lord in every situation.

## Stilling the Storm, 4:35–41

This incident is recorded in all three Synoptic Gospels, but Mark includes a number of details not found in the others. Some of these details are not essential to the story but are the sort of things an eyewitness would recall. Such

Fig. 5. First-century boat found in 1986 along the northwest shore of the Sea of Galilee, the sort of boat Jesus and the disciples used.

matters as the presence of other boats, the mention that Jesus was taken into the boat "just as He was," and Jesus sleeping on the cushion are found only in Mark. This is consistent with the understanding that Mark's writing was based on the preaching of the eyewitness Peter.[1]

"On that day" (v. 35) makes it clear that this event followed that extremely busy day of teaching in parables. Jesus asked the disciples to go with Him by boat to the "other side" of the lake. They had been on the northwest shore at Capernaum, and He proposed going to the east side, which was less populated and was actually outside of Galilee in Decapolis.

The puzzling phrase "just as He was" has been variously explained, but the most likely meaning is that He went somewhat abruptly, without any special preparation for the trip. The presence of the "other boats" provided more witnesses to the miracle, although that fact is not mentioned. One wonders what happened to them in the storm. Presumably they survived it and made it safely to shore after the miraculous calming of the waves.

Fierce storms are not unusual on the Sea of Galilee. Its waters lie more than 600 feet below sea level, and the lake is rimmed by mountains. As the sun begins to decline in the west, the winds rush down to the cooling surface, and the sea quickly becomes rough. Even experienced sailors find the waters dangerous, and many a fishing boat has been lost there. In 1986 one such boat from the first century was found near Ginosar,[2] and can be seen today in a museum at the kibbutz there.

---

[1]See Chapter 1, "Authorship of the Gospel," 2.
[2]Wachsmann, Shelley. *The Sea of Galilee Boat* (New York: Plenum Press, 1995).

Jesus, meanwhile, was sleeping in the stern of the boat. He must have been exhausted from His strenuous day, so that even the storm did not waken Him. The disciples, however, became so fearful and agitated that they woke Him with an implied rebuke, "Do You not care that we are perishing?" Only Mark includes the portion, "Do You not care?" Peter's memory of that momentous occasion doubtless caused him to mention it to Mark.

With amazing authority Jesus caused the winds to cease and the billowing of the waves to stop instantly. Some have noted that the words "rebuked" and "hush" (literately "be muzzled") sound like He is speaking with personal beings, and have suggested that the storm was instigated by demonic forces, but no real point is made of that here. More likely He was using this language somewhat figuratively to redirect the forces of nature.

Jesus then spoke to the disciples about their fears, which He explained as a lack of faith. They had been with Him long enough to recognize that He was the Son of God with the authority to accomplish everything He set out to do. Furthermore, He had told them to go with Him to the other side. They should have trusted Him to fulfill His plan, instead of falling victim to fearing for their lives.

As a result of this remarkable event, the disciples were awestruck, even though they had witnessed other miracles by Jesus and already believed He was divine. They needed to learn that their faith could still grow, and that their frailties in this regard would always need to be recognized.

# The Gerasene Man, 5:1–20

### The Man, 5:1–5

Jesus and the disciples crossed the Sea of Galilee to the eastern shore. The manuscripts at this point vary among the Synoptics, using the words "Gadarenes," "Gergasenes," or "Gerasenes." Today's consensus is to understand Matthew as using "Gadarenes," while Mark and Luke use "Gerasenes." The problem is that the story requires a seaside location, but the city of Gadara is located too far inland, and Gerasa (Jerash) is more than thirty miles south of the sea. Probably Matthew's use of "country of the Gadarenes" was meant to identify the locale with the territory of a major city. "Gerasenes," however, probably refers to the village of Kursi on the east shore of the Sea of Galilee. This is the only spot in the region where cliffs are along the shore and provide the appropriate setting for the pigs' stampede.

Jesus and His companions were swiftly brought back from the spiritual elation of the stilling of the storm to depressing human reality when they were confronted by a man possessed by evil spirits. This unfortunate fellow (along with a companion mentioned in Matthew) could not be housed safely among normal people, so he was living in a burial area. The tombs were often caves in the rocks, either natural or hewn, and he was living in empty ones for his shelter. His demon possession had provided him with unnatural strength, so that neither fetters for his feet nor chains on his arms could restrain him. He was like a wild beast at large in the region. At night he must have terrorized the countryside, frightening the inhabitants and injuring himself.

### The Meeting with Jesus, 5:6–10

The man's vision was sharp, and recognizing Jesus from a great distance, he ran and prostrated himself before Jesus in an imploring gesture of one seeking a favor. His outcry proves that the man was not insane but under demonic control, for he recognized Christ's identity as the Son of God (see Mark 3:31 for a previous instance of demonic recognition of Christ's deity). The demon knew full well that the coming of Christ meant certain doom for him. Therefore, his request was that the doom might be averted or at least delayed. In every encounter Jesus had with demons, they recognized Christ instantly and were obedient to His commands. His supernatural power extended to the spirit world as well as the world of men.

The demon-possessed man told Jesus his name was "Legion." The term "legion" referred to a division of the Roman army consisting at full strength of 6,000 men. To the resident of the country occupied by Rome's forces, the term would connote oppression as well as a large number. By asking his name, Jesus caused the man to look at himself and acknowledge his pitiful state.

It is difficult to tell in this conversation whether the man himself is speaking or the demon making use of the man's voice. The shift from singular to plural pronouns, *"My* name is Legion; for *we* are many," suggests that the personalities of the man and his demonic invaders had become so intertwined that absolute distinction is almost impossible for us to make. The demon (perhaps one of them being spokesman for the many) asked that Jesus would not send them away out of the country. Apparently the region in which they were now operating was open to their nefarious activity. Luke explains that what they feared was being sent to the abyss (that is, confinement in hell). Thus, they pleaded with Jesus that they might not be completely disembodied.

### The Miracle, 5:11–13

Near the scene where Jesus was dealing with the demon-possessed man was a herd of 2,000 swine. Many Gentiles lived in this region as well as Jews, so they may have been the owners. If not, then the owners were Jews who were violating their ceremonial law. (Perhaps this explains why they brought no legal action against Jesus for the loss.)

When they left the man, the demons asked permission to enter the swine. This was not disobedience to the command of Christ, for He had merely told them to leave the man (v. 8). The miracle was accomplished when the demons left

Fig. 6. Cliffs at Kursi (Gerasa) on east shore of the Sea of Galilee, where the swine rushed into the sea.

the man. They then entered into the pigs who promptly stampeded down a precipice and were all drowned in the sea. We should note that Jesus did not specifically order the demons to enter the swine. He merely permitted it. This did not make Him any more responsible for the resultant loss of the pigs than God is responsible for the evils which He permits in the world. The loss of such a large number of pigs indicated a large-scale neglect of Jewish law, and also could well have brought financial catastrophe to the owners.

### The People's Response, 5:14–17

The hired hands who had been tending the swine went immediately into the city and reported to all they encountered the strange things that had happened. This caused a number of curiosity-seekers to come to the scene. How surprised they were to see the demoniac in the presence of Jesus! Instead of roaming about as a wild man, he was sitting quietly. Rather than being naked (Luke 8:27), he was now covered. And in contrast to his former practice of shrieking insanely, he was in full possession of his mental faculties. This remarkable transformation produced fear in the onlookers—no longer a fear of the man, but an awe-filled respect in the presence of such supernatural power.

The witnesses of the event explained to the new arrivals what had happened. As a result, Jesus was requested to leave the community. His spiritual accomplishments were not as important to them as the disruption of their normal life pattern. Some may have feared more economic loss. Others doubtless felt uncomfortable in the presence of such awesome power and, being unwilling to yield their lives to God, preferred to let life go on as it had. They were awestruck but unrepentant. They remind us of many today who will tolerate religion only if it does not interfere with their worldly interests.

### The Man's Response, 5:18–20

Jesus never forced Himself upon those who did not want Him. Therefore, He prepared to leave at once by the boat in which He had arrived. The man who had been restored by Jesus did not share the attitude of the people, however, and he asked Jesus whether he might join Him, apparently as a disciple. One can understand his feelings.

Jesus did not accept his offer, but told him to remain where he was and be a witness in his home area. Our Lord did not desire that every believer become a part of His touring group, and those who acknowledged Him as Lord must recognize that the choice of who was to serve in one area and who in another belonged to Him and not to them. We need to remember this today. Each person must seek from the Lord the specific direction for his own life and must learn to distinguish, as this former demoniac did, the express will of the Lord from the more natural inclination of the heart.

The man had not only experienced alleviation of his satanic affliction but also must have become a true believer in Jesus. He accepted without question the lordship of Christ in his life and proceeded to carry out Christ's instructions with energy and effectiveness. His former notoriety made his witness especially impressive.

## Two Miracles: The Daughter of Jairus and the Woman with a Hemorrhage, 5:21–43

Miracles of raising the dead are commonly regarded as the most impressive displays of divine power in human life. This is probably because there is the clearest line of demarcation between life and death. In contrast to miracles of healing, no one can say that the victim of death might have recovered anyway. Thus, a miraculous raising always created a tremendous stir. Jesus raised only three persons during His ministry, and these three were each distinct. A progression can be noted: Jairus' daughter had just died. The son of the widow of Nain had been dead about a day (Luke 7:12; in that day and climate Jewish burials normally occurred on the day of death). Lazarus had been dead four days (John 11:39). Someday Christ will raise the dead of all ages (John 5:28–29).

### The Plea of Jairus, 5:21–24

When Jesus crossed the Sea of Galilee once again, He probably landed at Capernaum on the northwest shore. He was soon surrounded by a crowd of people and began to minister to their various needs. One man named Jairus implored Him to come to his home and touch his critically ill daughter. Since the Scripture writers do not name all the recipients of Jesus' miracles, it is attractive to speculate that perhaps this man was named because he was a believer and thus was known in the Church when the Gospel was first circulated.

On an earlier occasion when a centurion wanted Jesus to heal his servant in Capernaum, the Jewish officials interceded for him (Luke 7:3–5). One wonders whether Jairus had been one of those officials. After witnessing what Jesus had done for the Roman centurion, Jairus had good reason to ask the aid of Jesus for his own daughter.

### The Woman with a Hemorrhage, 5:25–34

*Her Condition, 5:25–26.* As Jesus was in the midst of the crowd, having just been asked to go to the house of Jairus, a woman worked her way to Him from behind and touched His clothing. This woman had suffered from her ailment for twelve years. The particular disease that caused this symptom is not named by any of the Gospel writers. The treatments that she had endured from various physicians during those years were even more painful than the ailment itself. In addition, she had spent all her savings and was now impoverished. To make matters worse, none of these efforts had brought improvement, but rather had caused her condition to deteriorate. (The physician Luke softens this last observation a bit by stating that she was incurable, Luke 8:43.) The Law of Moses pronounced such persons ceremonially unclean and forbade them from touching any other person (Lev. 15:19–30). Common tradition often regarded them as immoral, which of course was not necessarily true. There is nothing to indicate that the woman in this incident was an immoral person.

*Her Action, 5:27–28.* Matthew 9:20 specifies that she touched the fringe of His garment—perhaps the tassel worn by Jews at each of the four corners of the outer garment, in accordance with Numbers 15:39 and Deuteronomy 22:12. She believed that if she could merely touch His clothing, she would be restored. Although it is possible that she attached some superstitious reverence to the clothing, we should note that it was faith, not superstition, that brought the healing, for Jesus said so (v. 34).

*Her Cure, 5:29.* Immediately upon the touch, she was healed. There was no spoken word of Jesus. In fact, Jesus gave no indication that He knew of her presence prior to the miracle (although, of course, He may have known). Nevertheless, she was completely cured and somehow realized that her ailment was gone.

*Jesus' Response, 5:30–34.* Jesus may not have seen the woman's approach, but He was immediately aware that His spiritual power had been tapped. Clearly, then, the miracle was performed with the volition of Christ. The question He asked was thus not for information but to cause the woman to step forward and be acknowledged. She must not be allowed to feel that the miracle had been surreptitious. Furthermore, the private nature of her ailment, which made the cure not readily apparent, made some sort of public pronouncement of the healing necessary if she were to be freed from any social stigma.

With the natural reticence of Eastern women in the presence of men, she came trembling to Jesus and told the whole story. To her He said, "Your faith has made you well." It was her trust in Christ's power that brought healing. "Go in peace," He said. "Peace" is the Hebrew term which connotes prosperity and blessing. This woman received not only a physical cure but the pronouncement of spiritual salvation as well, as she looked in faith to Jesus the Messiah.

### The Death of Jairus' Daughter, 5:35–43

Before Jesus and the worried father Jarius could arrive at the home, word arrived that the daughter had died. Everyone thought that death had closed the door to any intervention from Jesus. Their advice was to stop bothering Jesus any further.

To the heartbroken man, Jesus offered the encouraging word, "Do not be afraid …only believe." Fear is the opposite of faith, for it refuses to trust God. Jesus knew what He was about to do and challenged Jairus to trust that He would do what was needed in this circumstance.

*The Scene at the Home, 5:37–38.* Peter, James, and John had accompanied Jairus to his home. This is the earliest of three instances in the Gospels in which Jesus selected these three for special experiences (the other occasions are the Transfiguration and Gethsemane). No reason is given as to why these particular three were chosen. Twelve may have been too many to crowd into a house already filled with mourners.

Arriving at the house, Jesus found a grieving crowd. Much of this was traditional at Eastern funerals. Professional mourners were often hired. Even though the loud confusion would not have seemed as out of place to Jairus as it does to us, it did make the ministration of Jesus more difficult. Therefore, He put a stop to it. By His question, "Why make a commotion and weep?" we understand that the mourning was excessive in this case.

*The Action of Jesus, 5:39–43.* Jesus said to them, "The child has not died, but is asleep." He did not mean that she wasn't really dead, but He spoke in light of what He was about to do. Because she would be raised soon, her time of death would be no longer than a nap. Of course, she had actually died in our usual understanding of death. (See a similar statement by Jesus in the case of Lazarus in John 11:11–14.) Any attempt to avoid seeing a miracle by calling this a coma does not really avoid a miracle, for the instantaneous cure would still be miraculous. Because the mourners knew she was physically dead, they laughed at Jesus' apparent naiveté.

He then sent all the others outside so that Jesus, the parents, and the three disciples were the only ones to witness the raising.

Our Lord spoke to the dead girl in the Aramaic language (the native tongue in Palestine), calling her "little girl." Mark has preserved the actual statement, probably learning it from Peter, who had witnessed the event and never forgot the emotion-packed words. The bare word of Jesus was all that was needed to accomplish her raising. The text says literally, "She was walking about," emphasizing that the action was continuous. One can visualize how this twelve-year-old girl must have darted from one parent to the other when she was restored. The great astonishment of the witnesses needs no comment. If anything, it is an understatement.

Jesus' command that there should be no publicizing of the event speaks volumes about His motives. A false prophet would have capitalized on it for all it was worth to gain a personal following. Jesus, however, desired no reputation as a mere wonder-worker. Nor did He want to give the impression that He would raise all the dead at this time. One can draw the conclusion that in this case He was moved primarily by the personal problems presented. His instruction that the girl be given something to eat indicates His concern even for a little girl's need. This miracle displayed both His sovereignty over life and death, and also the tender concern of God for human griefs and needs.

## Truths to Remember

• The miracles of Jesus display not only His power but also His love and grace.

• Christ's miracles should have led all who saw them to accept His message as from God, for they were fully consistent with God's previous revelation.

• Christ's almighty power did not prevent Him from being concerned about small needs. He not only concerned Himself with conquering death for a little girl and her grieving parents, but He also saw to it that she got some lunch. This indicates a great deal about the heart of God.

# 6

## ANOTHER TOUR OF GALILEE
### Mark 6:1–56

The earlier ministry of Jesus throughout Galilee had resulted in huge crowds of eager listeners and many instances of faith. This tour, however, will see the growth of opposition and more open displays of hostility.

### Visit to Nazareth, 6:1–6

Upon leaving Capernaum where the preceding miracles had occurred, Jesus made a visit to His hometown of Nazareth,[1] about twenty miles away in the mountains on the northern edge of the Jezreel Valley. He was accompanied by His disciples. Although some insist that He made just one visit to the synagogue at Nazareth,[2] it seems better to relate Luke 4:16–30 to an earlier visit and rejection in Nazareth.[3] Now He went to Nazareth again to give them another chance to receive Him.

The presence of Jesus teaching in the synagogue prompted some questioning and discussion among the townspeople. They were amazed at His wise instruction, as well as by the miracles that had been reported. "Is not this the carpenter?"

---

[1]Although Jesus was born in Bethlehem, Nazareth was where He had grown up. He was frequently called "Jesus of Nazareth" or "Jesus the Nazarene" (Mark 1:24; 10:47; 16:6).

[2]For example, Hendriksen, Wm., *Mark*, 220.

[3]Robertson, A. T. *A Harmony of the Gospels*, 77; Thomas, R. L. and S. N. Gundry, *A Harmony of the Gospels*, 94 ftn.

(v. 3). The expected answer to this question was yes. This is the only passage in the Gospels in which Jesus is called a carpenter. Elsewhere He was called "the carpenter's son" (Matt. 13:55). Of course, it was common for a son to learn the trade of his father. "The son of Mary" (v. 3) is an unusual designation, for normally a man is identified as the son of his father. Perhaps this is an indication that Joseph had died, although it still was more common in that culture to mention a man's father in identifying him, even if the father had died. Possibly it was a slur at Mary because of slanders circulating about the circumstances of Jesus' birth (cf. John 8:41).

Of the four brothers, James would appear to be the oldest. He later became prominent as the leader of the Jerusalem church (Acts 15:13; Gal. 1:19), and writer of the Epistle of James. Judas is also known as Jude, and later wrote the Epistle of Jude. We know nothing further of the remaining two brothers or the sisters. At the time of this visit of Jesus to Nazareth, however, none of the brothers was a believer in His mission (John 7:5). The prevailing view of His townsmen was that there was nothing extraordinary about Jesus, and thus they rejected His reputation and His claims.

Jesus recognized their skepticism and answered it with a proverb, "A prophet is not without honor except in his home town and among his own relatives and in his own household" (v. 4). He had used this same proverb earlier in John 4:44 when He left Samaria to go to Galilee, knowing that He would not receive an easy reception there, such as had previously happened in Jerusalem (John 2:23–25). Possibly Jesus originated this proverb. We have a similar proverb: Familiarity breeds contempt.

Jesus could not perform many miracles at Nazareth because of the people's unbelief. It was not that unbelief could hamper His power, but that unbelief restrained many from coming to Him for healing. Christ did not ordinarily perform miracles upon people unless they had enough faith to come to Him. His miracles were not mere entertainment or crowd builders. They were inherently connected with His message, and when people were insensitive to His message, there was no opportunity for more miracles. Therefore, He left Nazareth and began another tour of the villages of Galilee.

## Sending Out the Twelve, 6:7–13

Mark's Gospel is the only one to mention that Jesus sent out the Twelve in groups of two. The words, "Began to send them out (v. 7)" suggest the start of a procedure that would continue into the future. Such a method not only provided a means to have six separate places of preaching simultaneously, but it also offered a corroboration of the witness at each site, as well as mutual support for the disciples themselves. The Twelve were empowered to deal with unclean spirits, just as Jesus had been doing. Thus they were His fully authorized representatives.

The Twelve received instruction for this trip. Comparison with the Matthew and Luke parallels reveals several differences, particularly regarding a staff and sandals. Hendriksen has a helpful discussion.[4] A staff was used by every traveler. The Twelve were simply to use the one they already had, and were not to go out and acquire a new one (Matt. 10:10). The same was true regarding sandals. They should use what they had but not take along an extra pair. As for the remaining items Jesus mentioned, the principle

[4]Hendriksen, *op. cit*, 227–228.

was simply that they should not take along extras, not even an extra tunic, but trust God and accept the hospitality that would be afforded them.

As visiting religious teachers, they could expect to be invited into homes during their stay. In doing so, they should remain where they were first invited and not try to better themselves if a more attractive invitation were given. Time should not be wasted in moving about from one home to another.

If, however, they would be rejected in any place, they were to leave and perform the act of shaking off the dust from their feet as a symbolic gesture of complete disassociation from the fate of those who reject. This would testify to the townspeople the importance of their message and the seriousness of their rejection. (The Gospel of Matthew gives a much more extended record of Jesus' instruction (Matt. 10:1–42).

The Twelve proceeded to carry out the mission on which Christ sent them. They proclaimed that people needed to repent of sin and confess their need and readiness for Messiah. They also were effective in casting out demons, and anointed with oil many who were sick. This is the first mention of the use of oil in this way in the New Testament. Although olive oil was used medicinally in the Old Testament and in contemporary times, it seems more likely this instance was similar to James 5:14–15. The use of oil as a medicine was not employed for all ailments and was gradual in its effects when it was applied, not instantaneous with a miraculous sort of ministry as implied here. It was a commonly understood symbol of the presence and blessing of God, and points to God's agency in these healings through His Spirit.

A final report of this mission of the Twelve is given in verse 30. Mark, however, includes a report of the action of Herod Antipas, which is sandwiched in this account of the Twelve's mission. Mark did something similar in his inclusion of the woman with the hemorrhage episode within the account of raising the daughter of Jairus (Mark 5:22–43).

## The Fears of Herod Antipas, 6:14–29

The "King Herod" of verse 14 is actually Herod Antipas, tetrarch of Galilee and Perea and a son of Herod the Great. Although he was commonly referred to as king, it was more of a courtesy title for him, and he never was actually appointed as king by Rome. Later, in A.D. 39, he was deposed.

This narrative about King Herod may have been introduced into the account at this point because it was the increased preaching of the Twelve regarding Jesus that had come to Herod's attention. Herod seemed to know very little about Jesus, but he had thought highly of John the Baptist, even though it was Herod who had killed him. The notion that Jesus was a resurrected John reveals that Herod did not seem to know that John had baptized Jesus, or that the two of them were on the earth together before John's death. Other suggestions about Jesus' identity were prevalent, including a return of Elijah (based on Mal. 4:5), or some other Old Testament prophet. Herod, however, adopted the most startling of the suggestions, doubtless because of his own guilty conscience about John.

Mark then gives a historical flashback to explain what Herod Antipas had done to John some months before. His account is longer, more detailed, and more dramatic than Matthew's (Matt. 14:3–12), leading one to describe Mark "as a story-teller…unsurpassed among the four."[5] He explained that Herod Antipas had John arrested and imprisoned because

[5]Hendriksen, *op. cit.*, 236.

John had stated that Herod had unlawfully married Herodias, the former wife of Antipas' brother Philip. This accusation infuriated Herodias, and she wanted John put to death, but Antipas was not willing to go that far. In fact, he enjoyed summoning the imprisoned John and listening to him.

On Herod's birthday, Herodias saw her chance. At his birthday feast with many dignitaries present, the daughter of Herodias (at her mother's instigation, no doubt) performed a dance that greatly pleased Herod and his guests. The fact that the dinner guests were probably inebriated by this time, the dance was doubtless lewd or at least suggestive, and the disgrace associated with a princess acting in such a way, marked the entire episode as degraded. This daughter[6] probably learned the art while living in Rome with Herodias and Philip. Moved by the dance and no doubt by the wine, Herod fell into the trap laid for him by his wife and swore to give the girl whatever she asked, up to half of his kingdom. This last part of his offer was certainly an exaggeration, for as a tetrarch Herod was not a real king and could never fulfill such a grandiose promise. Nor did the girl ask for it.

Instead, the daughter asked her mother what she should ask for. Apparently the girl did not know at this point what her mother had in mind. However, there was no hesitation reflected in the mother's prompt answer, "Ask for the head of John the Baptist." The daughter showed no distaste whatever for her gory request, and immediately told Herod she wanted John's head on a platter. Was the mention of a platter a deliberate reference to the banquet setting? Although the request was distasteful to Herod because he knew John was a righteous man and he did not wish to offend his

---

[6]The first century historian Josephus gives her name as Salome. Josephus, *Antiquities*, 18.5.4.

conscience further, in his confused state he could think of no way to break his promise in front of so many distinguished guests. Therefore, he sent an executioner to the prison and had John beheaded. Josephus states that the place of John's imprisonment was at Machaerus in Perea,[7] and the birthday banquet must have been in the palace there in view of what follows. Many from Galilee were present at this banquet because of the birthday celebration to which Herod had invited them. The head of John the Baptist was duly brought to the banquet hall and given on a platter to the girl, who then gave it to her mother. The girl displays no squeamishness at this bizarre event, revealing a moral callousness as flagrant as her mother's.

John's disciples were his followers who had accepted his message and still had an attachment to him. Many of them had already joined Jesus, but some still remained with John. They were given permission to give a decent burial to their fallen leader. This sad episode that Herod Antipas carried out regarding John the Baptist lay in the background of Herod's new fears about Jesus and His ministry mentioned in verse 14.

## Feeding the Five Thousand, 6:30–44

When the Twelve apostles returned from their mission, they reported their experiences. This was the first tour they had taken without Jesus. It was obvious to Him that they were exhausted from their grueling pace, for they had not even had time to eat at normal hours. Consequently, He directed them to join Him privately for a time of seclusion by boat. Luke tells us that the location was near Bethsaida

[7]Josephus, *op. cit.*, 8.119.2.

Julias on the east side of the Jordan river, just north of where it enters the Sea of Galilee (Luke 9:10).

At Capernaum, the place where Jesus and the Twelve had been, people could see them depart by boat and could watch their progress along the north shore. People from many of the villages around Capernaum began to follow along the shore, and some may have arrived at Jesus' destination before He did (Mark 6:33). They would have had to cross the Jordan River to get there, but the distance was not far. Mark implies that some of them actually got there before the boat did, but most of the crowd arrived later during the day (John 6:5). Jesus and the Twelve may have had a short time of seclusion before the crowds arrived, but not much. The compassion of Jesus caused Him to abandon private time with His disciples so He could teach the multitudes of people.

Late in the day the disciples came to Jesus urging Him to dismiss the crowds so that they could go to the surrounding villages and buy food for themselves. John's Gospel indicates that Jesus had raised the problem earlier in the day so that they might think about it, but apparently they could come up with no solution (John 6:5). Jesus, however, indicated that the disciples should supply the food. The Twelve saw no way they could do this. How could they carry back from neighboring villages enough food for 5,000 men? Furthermore, how could they pay for it? It would take at least 200 denarii (equivalent to eight months' wages for a laboring man) to make the purchase, and this was far beyond what the disciples had available. Jesus then asked them to find out what food was available, and they reported they had five loaves and two fish (only John reports that this small quantity belonged to one lad). The Lord had made them recognize the enormity of the problem and thus the greatness of the forthcoming miracle.

The timing of this event was shortly before the springtime feast of Passover (John 6:4), and the grass was still green from the winter rains (Mark 6:39). The crowd formed groups of 50 and 100, and this made distribution easier and aided in counting the total number. Jesus offered prayer before the meal, as any pious Jew would, and then began to dispense the food. The miracle itself is not described, but it seems to have occurred between the breaking and the giving of it.[8] He broke the five breadcakes and continued to give the resulting pieces to the Twelve; He did likewise with the fish. No attempt is made by Mark to explain the unexplainable.

When all were fed and satisfied, twelve baskets were filled with the remainder, enough for each of the Twelve. These containers were the small wicker baskets in which each man carried his provisions. Thus Jesus made exactly enough for the crowd and the Twelve. It has been noticed that He made none for Himself. Apparently the Twelve were to share theirs with Him.

All four of the Gospels note that the crowd consisted of 5,000 males. It is commonly suggested that the number refers to family heads, so that when wives and children are added, the total would be more than twice that number. However, in all likelihood, the crowd was predominantly men, for women in that society would not usually have been as free to spend such a leisurely day. John reports that the crowd was minded to take Jesus by force and make Him king (John 6:15), and this might explain why all the Gospel writers stated that the crowd consisted of men only. (Even Matt. 14:21 can be understood as "five thousand men… without women and children [being present].") Were many

---

[8]This is the only miracle of Jesus recorded in all four Gospels (see Matt. 14:15–21; Luke 9:12–17; John 6:4–13).

of them Zealots whose anger had increased because of John the Baptist's recent execution by Antipas?

## Walking on Water, 6:45–56

Following the miraculous feeding of the five thousand, Jesus instructed the disciples to leave by boat while He went alone into the mountains to pray. As mentioned above, John indicates that the crowds desired to make Him king by force (John 6:15). Probably He wanted to protect the Twelve from being influenced to join that effort.

Jesus told the Twelve to go on ahead to Bethsaida (v. 45). This presents a problem because Luke has recorded that the feeding of the five thousand occurred at Bethsaida (Luke 9:10). If they were already at Bethsaida, how could they be instructed to go there? Some have harmonized this awkwardness by suggesting that the miraculous feeding took place in the countryside south of Bethsaida Julias, and that Jesus now directed them to head back to Galilee by way of Bethsaida Julias, perhaps using it as a stopping place for the night although the wind blew them off course.[9] More commonly, however, it is explained as indicating another Bethsaida in Galilee, a fishing village suburb of Capernaum.[10] Whichever view is correct is somewhat immaterial, because the boat never made it to that place, and instead landed at Gennesaret (v. 53; Matt. 14:34).

As the disciples embarked, Jesus went into the mountain to pray in privacy. He spent that stormy night in communion with the Father, probably in response to the crucial issues of that day and the one to follow.

[9]For example, Swift, C. E. Graham, "Mark," *New Bible Commentary* (Grand Rapids: Eerdmans, 1958), 819.
[10]R. L. Thomas and S. N. Gundry, *loc. cit.*, 101 ftn.

Fig. 7. Site of Gennesaret, near Capernaum on the northwest shore of the Sea of Galilee.

Meanwhile the disciples were about three and a half miles off shore (John 6:19), roughly halfway across the lake, when Jesus observed them rowing with great difficulty because of the developing storm. By this time it was the fourth watch of the night (between 3:00 a.m. and 6:00 a.m. Roman reckoning). Miraculously, Jesus approached them walking on the water. "He intended to pass by them" (v. 48). This feature of the narrative is not mentioned by Matthew or John, and therefore it must not have impressed those two eyewitnesses as significant. Perhaps He was planning to lead them to shore, or was waiting for them to invite Him onboard. But from the perspective of the disciples, it looked as if He were going to pass by. At first they thought they were seeing a ghost, and they cried out in fear. Not just a few of them were terrified; all of them were (v. 50). Jesus then identified Himself, urged them to stop fearing, and came on board the boat. The wind immediately stopped, to the great astonishment of the disciples.

Mark omits any mention of Peter's walking on the water (see Matt. 14:28–31). This may have been because of Peter's reluctance to talk about himself (on the assumption that Mark's Gospel is a faithful reflection of Peter's preaching on the subject), or Mark's sensitivity to Peter's shortcomings on that occasion (although Matthew showed no hesitation!). John's Gospel does not mention this incident either.

The astonishment of the disciples (v. 51) is explained as a lack of understanding of Jesus' power over nature, even though they had just witnessed the stupendous multiplication of five loaves and two fish, and had seen Him calm another storm only a few months earlier (Mark 4:35–41). But their hearts were "hardened" (v. 52), and they were not as sensitive to what was occurring as they should have been.

The boat with Jesus and the Twelve put ashore at Gennesaret, a few miles beyond Capernaum along the north shore of the Sea of Galilee. Inasmuch as John's Gospel puts Jesus in Capernaum on the day after the storm (John 6:22–59), we must understand that Mark is giving a summary of what went on during these days. He must have gone directly to Capernaum upon disembarking.

Verses 54–56 describe in summary the events of the next few days or weeks. The interest of the people was not on hearing His message but on bringing sick people to Him for healing. Their trust in His power was so great that they believed even the slightest physical contact with Him would be enough to heal them. Doubtless the experience of the woman with the hemorrhage who touched Jesus' garment had been reported in the area (Mark 5:27–28). Christ honored this simple faith with healing.

## Truths to Remember

• When we refuse to believe Jesus can help us, He probably won't.

• Even Jesus needed to rest and to pray.

• Jesus is Lord of the natural world, just as He wants to be of our lives.

# 7

## EXCURSIONS AROUND AND OUTSIDE GALILEE – I
### Mark 7:1–37

Mark's discussion about ceremonial defilement as opposed to true spiritual defilement is not found in Luke or John but is paralleled in Matthew. The fact that Mark's Gospel is probably based on Peter's preaching, as the earliest Christian writers stated, is interesting in light of Peter's own problems with this concept. It took a voice from heaven coupled with a vision of a sheet with all kinds of animals in it before Peter, even as a Christian, would go into a Gentile's house and eat with him (Acts 10: 1–48). Later, however, at Antioch he wavered regarding Jewish eating practices and went against his better knowledge, bringing down upon himself a rebuke from Paul (Gal. 2:11–17). Eventually he learned the truth of what Jesus meant, and proclaimed it clearly as Mark has recorded.

The question of how men ought to live has always been a perplexing one, with no lack of suggested answers. Whether or not one is a Christian, he usually will recognize that all people are imperfect in some degree, and those who recognize that mankind has a responsibility to God are usually willing to call their failures sin. Thus, most religious systems involve some sort of purification, whether in ceremony or in theological teaching. But what makes humans sinful? Are they such things as worldly pleasures, immoral living, and evil deeds? Are these really the source of our unholiness before God, or merely symptoms of a more basic cause?

People often confuse the cause with the symptoms. Throughout history there have been ascetics who have tried to avoid spiritual defilement by withdrawing from contact with the world. Hermits and monks of various sorts are examples of this approach. Others have thought that evil resided in physical objects, so that the secret of holiness was to compile a list of taboos and refrain from any indulgence in these specified items. The drawing up of such a list, however, is a most subjective matter, and rarely do any two lists agree. This is legalism.

Another view explains defilement as inherent in the physical body. According to this philosophy, one needs to treat his physical body with the utmost austerity and thereby starve out its appetites and passions. All kinds of variations exist within these types, and they serve to emphasize the truth that the problem of human defilement is as wide as the human race and that most of our attempts at a solution have been inadequate.

Now, this whole matter has more than a mere academic interest. It matters a great deal how we understand sin and its causes. Unless we learn the source of the problem, no treatment of symptoms will ever cure the disease. Jesus had a great deal to say about the matter of defilement. His answer to the problem is just as relevant today as when He first addressed the Pharisees.

## Discussion about Defilement, 7:1–23

### The Complaint, 7:1–5

A complaint about defilement was raised by some Pharisees and scribes who had come from Jerusalem to

Galilee. Scribes were professional teachers and interpreters of the Scripture. Pharisees were members of a religious party noted for its orthodoxy both in relation to Mosaic Law and also to rabbinical tradition. Unfortunately, they had come to rely so heavily upon rabbinical interpretations with their rules and regulations for observing the Law that sometimes the Mosaic Law was obscured and violated. It often happens that when people hold to God's Word *and* something else, the something else takes prominence and God's Word becomes secondary.

Mark's mention that they "came from Jerusalem" (v. 1) was not for the purpose of merely naming their place of residence, but to indicate that they had just come to Galilee, apparently on this specific mission. They had doubtless been sent by the religious leaders in Jerusalem in order to investigate Jesus and trap Him in some violation of religious law. The leaders in Jerusalem had already begun plotting to do away with Jesus (John 5:18). Their opportunity came when they saw some of our Lord's disciples take food without going through the elaborate ritual of washing their hands. The problem was not hygienic but ceremonial.

Verse 3 indicates that this practice, which was observed so scrupulously by the Pharisees, was also followed by Jews generally. It was not, however, a rule contained in the Old Testament. It was a part of the 613 rabbinical rules that had been added by Jewish leaders in subsequent years. Ostensibly, these traditional rules of the elders were supposed to be a safeguard for the Law. By keeping them, the Jew would not inadvertently transgress some portion of the law of God. However, there were many times when just the opposite result occurred, as Jesus pointed out in the succeeding verses.

Fig. 8. First-century mikvah, or Jewish ritual bath, used for
ceremonial purification upon entering the temple.

The word "carefully" has been a problem for translators.
The best manuscripts say "with fist." Probably it denoted
an energetic and thorough washing with the fist of one
hand rubbed against the palm of the other. The practice was
extended by many pious Jews to include the washing not only
of themselves, but also of various material objects. Whenever
one returned home from the crowded marketplace, he was
expected to regard himself as ceremonially defiled and in
need of this ritualistic washing.

The delegation from Jerusalem made their complaint to
Jesus. They mentioned only the transgression of the disciples,
not any violation by Jesus. However, it seems clear that their
real complaint was against Jesus, for they inferred that He
was to blame. They called the men "Your" disciples and
registered their complaint with Jesus, not with the offenders.
They had drawn the conclusion that the disciples' action was

the result of their Master's teaching. According to their view, defilement of a spiritual sort had resulted from failure to observe these rabbinic washings. Through physical contact with "unclean" Gentiles or other ceremonially contaminated persons, one would stain his soul.

Now, the Mosaic Law did specify certain washings for ceremonial purposes. These observances were of great instructive value in pointing out God's holiness and man's constant need to walk in accord with His righteous demands. But it was possible to miss the point and suppose that material objects were sinful per se and that holiness could be achieved merely by avoiding physical contact. What was so easily forgotten was that sin is essentially a spiritual problem. People today still tend to emphasize things and deeds as sinful without recognizing that the real problem lies deeper.

**The Real Problem, 7:6–13**

*The Problem Stated, 7:6–8.* Jesus said that the attitude of these Pharisean critics was precisely what Isaiah had described in Isaiah 29:13.[1] This characterization of Israel was true not only of Isaiah's generation, but also of the nation throughout her history, and was just as true of Christ's contemporaries. By asserting that the people paid meticulous attention to rites and ceremonies ("honors Me with their lips," v. 6a), He called attention to their emphasis on the externals. But by noting there was an absence of spiritual, heartfelt religion ("their heart is far away from Me," v. 6b), Jesus declared that they were guilty of hypocrisy. They really did not mean what their acts of worship declared. Their problem was the condition of their hearts, which no amount of external rites could rectify.

[1]The quotation is taken from the Septuagint (LXX), and differs somewhat from the Hebrew text (MT). The point is the same, however, in both texts.

The basic idea of "hypocrisy" is pretense. The Greek term *hypokrites* was used of an actor who wore a mask and portrayed a part other than his normal self. It is possible for religious forms to hide a most unspiritual heart. Religious forms are not necessarily wrong. God's Word prescribed many of them in the Old Testament and some in the New Testament. But men must make certain that the forms are the demonstration of a true heart and not a mask to hide an evil one.

The quotation from Isaiah went on to say that human regulations had been substituted for the truth of God. These human additions (in this case, the rabbinical rules about defilement) had resulted in a worship that was in vain. Instead of enabling the worshiper to obey God more perfectly, these rules had taken attention away from men's hearts and focused it on externals. As a consequence, spiritual condition was glossed over by a veneer of practices. What may have once been regarded as a helpful rule had become an instrument of disobedience.

*The Problem Illustrated, 7:9–13.* Doubtless a great many of the traditional practices lacked any real spiritual implications. Where the spiritual element of worship was absent, the practices had become empty forms but not positive evils. In some instances, however, they came into direct conflict with God's commandments. Yet, even in such situations these tradition-bound people gave the preference to human tradition and ignored their obligation to God.

One glaring example was described by Jesus. The Mosaic Law was absolutely clear on the principle that children should give their parents due respect. This not only involved obedience when the children were small but also provision for their parents in old age. Such passages as Exodus 20:12 and Deuteronomy 5:16 declare this obligation. It became a part of Jewish culture and is reiterated in the New Testament as well (Eph. 6:1–3, 1 Tim. 5:4). Furthermore, the Old Testament law actually imposed the death penalty upon those who reviled either parent (Ex. 21:17).

The Jews of Jesus' day had found a way to circumvent this divine obligation. Rabbinical law allowed a person to donate money or goods to God or to the temple by designating the donation as "Corban" (that is, "gift"). Anything so designated became sacred and thus could not be used or sold for any other purpose. By this stratagem, it was not an uncommon practice for Jews to avoid their temporal obligations by piously claiming that the money (or goods) involved had been dedicated to God. When aged and needy parents appealed to such a son for help, he would say, "Sorry, my money has been dedicated to God." One wonders how promptly the money would then be turned over to the priests. Doubtless there were many abuses, but that is not the point here. Jesus is not blaming these men for failing to give the money to God. He is pointing out that God does not want from a man what should be used for the care of his parents. They had allowed man-made procedures to cause them to violate the direct commandment of God regarding the honoring of parents. The rabbinical law reserved such gifts for the temple so rigidly that no amount of pleading on the part of indigent parents could free that money for their aid.

Jesus also said that the above instance was by no means the only example. What they were actually doing was elevating human tradition above scriptural commands. When the two came into conflict, the rabbinical law was followed, and thus the authority of Scripture was ignored.

The people whom Jesus addressed had gotten into these corrupt practices because their hearts were defiled. When they claimed "Corban" to avoid assisting their parents, it was because of greed, not piety. It was the result of ingratitude toward the parents, not thanksgiving to God. In essence it was because of a heart that was either ignorant of, or rebellious against, the clear revelation of God. This is the basic element in all sin—refusal to accept God's will and insistence upon one's own.

### The Source of Defilement, 7:14–23

At this point Jesus wanted to speak not only to the scribes and Pharisees but also to the larger crowd of His followers. Perhaps they had withdrawn in the presence of these visiting dignitaries. Now Jesus called them back to Him so that they, too, could benefit from the truth of these teachings. These were vital issues that all men needed to know.

Jesus explained that nothing from the outside of a man can defile him. Only those things that originate from within can do so. He was not at this point abrogating the distinctions made in Levitical law between clean and unclean things. But He was explaining that physical items per se cannot cause spiritual defilement. Even Levitical impurity was actually the result of the condition of the heart that disobeyed God's law, rather than merely the partaking of certain foods. A Jew was defiled when he ate pork, not because pork was evil but because he was disobeying a specific commandment from God. Defilement comes from the hearts of sinful men. The error of the Jews was shifting the blame from the internal to the external. By codifying their duties, they had nullified the basic spiritual truths.

Later, when the crowds had gone and Jesus was alone in a house with His disciples, He was asked about the meaning of His previous statements. "Are you so lacking in understanding also?" asked Jesus. Because they had been ingrained with the traditional Jewish attitude toward external rites, they failed to comprehend what Jesus meant. The same mistake of equating defilement with external things is often still made.

Jesus then rehearsed what He had said with even more detail. He showed that material things cannot defile the spirit. Spiritual defilement is caused by spiritual attitudes. The reason food cannot defile the heart of a man is that it does not enter his heart, his moral center. A literal translation of verse 19a is, "Because it goes not into his heart but into the belly, and goes out into the latrine." Foods, therefore, are physically important, but not morally significant, and are eventually disposed of. The closing part of verse 19 is rightly understood as Mark's comment on Jesus' statement and is placed in parentheses in NASB: "Thus He declared all foods clean." When this Gospel was written for Gentile readers, probably in Rome, this principle was already well established and understood. It clearly reflects the instruction given to Peter in the vision on the housetop: "What God has cleansed, no longer consider unholy" (Acts 10:15). At the time Jesus spoke, however—about a year before the crucifixion, resurrection, and establishment of the Christian church—ceremonial distinctions were still in place in the Levitical law for Jews. The point Jesus had been making was that the things that were ritualistically unclean were not inherently evil in themselves. Some Jews were confusing ritual taboos with moral evils.

True defilement is spiritual and moral. It proceeds from the inner being of man, which is sinful by nature. Jesus then gave a series of examples of spiritual defilement, which originate within the heart of man. "Evil thoughts" (v. 21) are not only ideas but also purposes and schemes. In the New Testament this word for "thoughts" is always used in a bad sense. "Fornications" refers to illicit acts of sex among the unmarried. "Adulteries" refers to illicit sex among those already married.

"Murders" and "thefts," of course, are acts of taking another's life or property. "Deeds of coveting" is plural, thus meaning acts of covetousness, not merely an attitude. But all of the above-named actions begin with evil thoughts in the heart.

"Wickedness, deceit, sensuality" are various sorts of flagrant, wanton behavior contrary to the moral law of God. "Envy" (Greek: *ophthalmos ponēros,* lit. "an evil eye") denotes a feeling of jealousy because of what someone else does (see Matt. 20:15 for a similar use of this phrase). "Slander" is injurious speech, whether against men or God. "Pride" and "foolishness" are not acts, but attitudes; they are also evil and contaminate the heart of the man who has them.

Verse 23 summarizes by restating the principle that the previous verses have illustrated. What really defiles a man and renders him unholy is to be traced to an unclean heart. As Jeremiah 17:9 says, "The heart is more deceitful than all else, and is desperately sick: Who can understand it?"

## Exorcism of a Demon-Possessed Girl in Syrophoenicia, 7:24–30

### The Place, 7:24

Jesus left the territory of the Jews and went northwest to the region of Phoenicia (present day Lebanon), where the principal cities were Tyre and Sidon. This was purely Gentile country, and was apparently the only time in Jesus' ministry in which He made such an excursion outside the historical borders of Israel. It should be clear that His purpose was not to do foreign missionary work, but to find seclusion from the crowds and an opportunity for private instruction of the Twelve. Therefore, He entered a house and tried to keep His presence secret. However, His reputation had spread even to this foreign land.

### The Plea, 7:25–26

Christ's fame had preceded Him to the region, so that the moment a certain woman heard of His arrival, she went to Him with her plea. The woman was a Greek (that is, a Gentile), born in Phoenicia, which was now governed by Syria. Her daughter was possessed by an evil spirit, and the mother came pleading for assistance. The verb "kept asking" (v. 26) notes the repeated request she made. This woman was in earnest.

### The Explanation, 7:27

Using an illustration from domestic life, Jesus said, "Let the children be satisfied first." He explained His policy of confining His earthly preaching ministry to Jews, who are here referred to as children. The reason was not that He had no interest in Gentiles but that by fulfilling the Old Testament promises to the Jews, He would be making possible the blessing of all nations by the Jews' proclamation of the Gospel. (The first Christians were Jews who then became the first missionaries.) "First" implies that there would be others to be fed next.

When Jesus said it was not good to take the bread of the children and throw it to the dogs, the statement was probably not as harsh as it sounds to us. Although "dogs" was a common expression of the Jews to denote Gentiles, the word here was "little dogs." It connoted not the vicious scavengers of the street but the household pets of the children. The average Jew regarded all Gentiles as unclean and avoided contact with them if at all possible. Under no circumstances would an average Jew have felt obliged to assist this Gentile woman. He would have thought such contact to be defiling. On the contrary, even though a Gentile ministry was not Christ's present program, He did not regard her as one to be avoided. He was willing to listen, and eventually to help.

### The Insistence, 7:28

The woman made no objection to what Jesus said. She accepted His explanation of His procedure, but she also requested His aid as an isolated act of His ministry. "But, even the [little] dogs under the table feed on the children's crumbs," she said. She asked if there could not be at least a "crumb" of His blessing available for her, even though as a Gentile it was not God's plan that she be entitled to a place at the "table" just yet.

### The Miracle, 7:29–30

The insistence of the woman showed her faith, and the way she replied indicated her submission to Christ's explanation of His ministry. In view of this faith, Jesus granted her request. No word of command for the miracle was given. He merely stated that the child was cured. And upon the mother's return home, she found her daughter in repose, resting from her torments. How glad this mother was that Jesus did not think that contact with a Gentile would defile Him and thus prevent His ministry!

## Healing of a Deaf and Dumb Man in Decapolis, 7:31–37

This miracle is described only in Mark's Gospel, although Matthew gives a few generalizing sentences to summarize Christ's ministry at this particular time (Matt. 15:29–31). From the scene of the last episode in the vicinity of Tyre, Jesus moved about twenty-five miles north to Sidon, and then on a circuit to the east side of the Sea of Galilee in Decapolis. This was an extensive journey that probably would have taken several months. He was clearly outside of Galilee at this time.

At some unidentified place, a deaf and dumb man was brought to Jesus. In this instance Jesus took the man aside in order to meet his needs apart from the distractions of the crowd. The man's difficulty seems to be physical in nature, not a case of demon possession. Consequently, He touched the two affected members so that the man would recognize what Jesus was about to do for him. Putting His fingers in the man's ears, and using saliva on His finger, He touched his tongue. Jesus then prayed with a sigh, perhaps an expression of His sympathy with the man's affliction, and spoke one word in Aramaic (the language of the ailing man?), which Mark translated into Greek for his readers: "Be opened." That simple statement (one word in Greek) produced the miracle. Immediately the healing effects were produced, and the crowds were astonished. Such miracles were rather commonplace for Jesus in Galilee and Judea, but may have been new to this region.

Once again Jesus cautioned the man and the witnesses not to spread the word about this healing, although Mark gives no reason. Presumably the people of this area, not being as acquainted with Jesus, could easily become overly excited and miss the spiritual aspect of His ministry. Unfortunately, His efforts to keep down the publicity failed to silence the people. When Mark notes the comments of the people regarding what had happened, he does so in words that echoed the messianic prophecy of Isaiah 35:5–6: "Then the eyes of the blind will be opened, and the ears of the deaf will be unstopped. Then the lame will leap like a deer, and the tongue of the dumb will shout for joy." These were significant times in God's Messianic program.

## Truths to Remember

• We usually find it more convenient to condemn sins we can see than the hidden sins of the heart.

• True defilement comes out of hearts that are not right before God.

• Sometimes wrong notions about defilement keep us from doing the things God desires of us.

• When human traditions are added to God's Word, the Word usually takes second place.

# 8

# EXCURSIONS AROUND AND OUTSIDE GALILEE – II
## Mark 8:1–38

## Feeding Four Thousand, 8:1–9

The similarities between the narratives of the feedings of the 5,000 and the 4,000 have caused most liberal scholars to conclude these are simply two versions of one event.[1] Mark, however, clearly understood them as separate. He also quoted Jesus as referring to them separately (8:18–20), as does Matthew (16:9–10). One's view of inspiration must be very low to allow for a single-event interpretation.

It has also been noted that Mark has used a certain pattern in structuring this portion of his Gospel. An interesting parallelism occurs in the arrangement of events in chapters 6:31 to 8:30. This arrangement can be clearly seen in Chart 8.1, given by Lane and others.[2]

Mark does not comment on this feature in his text, and there is no problem with such an arrangement by him. We do not know what his purpose was. Perhaps the feeding of the

---

[1]For example, Mann, C. S., *Mark* in *The Anchor Bible* series (Garden City, NY: Doubleday & Co., 1986), 325.

[2]Lane, Wm., *The Gospel According to Mark*, 269; also Wessel, Walter, "Mark," *The Expositor's Bible Commentary*, VIII, 686; Brooks, James A., *Mark* in *The New American Commentary*, Vol. 23, 124.

**Chart 8.1**

| | | |
|---|---|---|
| Ch. 6:31–44 | Feeding of the Multitude | Ch. 8:1–9 |
| Ch. 6:45–56 | Crossing of the Sea and Landing | Ch. 8:10 |
| Ch. 7:1–23 | Conflict with the Pharisees | Ch. 8:11–13 |
| Ch. 7:24–30 | Conversation about Bread | Ch. 8:14–21 |
| Ch. 7:31–36 | Healing | Ch. 8:22–26 |
| Ch. 7:37 | Confession of Faith | Ch. 8:27–30 |

5,000 and the events that followed, which occurred in Galilee, involved a Jewish audience and showed their response to the power of Jesus. On the other hand, the feeding of the 4,000 and the following events in Decapolis involved a mostly Gentile audience, and one is able to compare their response to the Jewish one. At the very least Mark (and Matthew) enable us to see that Christ's interest in Gentiles existed during His ministry, even though He was sent first to the "lost sheep of the house of Israel" (Matt. 10:6).

"In those days" (v. 1) places the setting in Decapolis, just as the foregoing event. This was a less populated region than Galilee, and the location of Jesus and the multitudes was not close to any place where food could be obtained. These people had been with Jesus for three days (v. 2), and their supplies had run out. Christ felt compassion for their physical needs and did not want to send them away hungry, because their travel distance would be too great for their depleted strength.

The disciples' question to Jesus, "Where will anyone be able to find enough to satisfy these men with bread here in a desolate place?" (v. 4), seems to show a remarkable shortness of memory on their part. They had witnessed His feeding of the 5,000 just a few months before. R. C. H. Lenski suggests that the disciples did not mean to include Jesus in "anyone," so they meant that the project of supplying bread for this crowd was beyond their capability. It would be up to Jesus to take care of it, just as He had done before.[3]

Jesus asked the disciples what food they had available, and their reply was that only seven loaves of bread (v. 5) and a few small fish (v. 7) were left, presumably from what they themselves had brought along. He then directed that the crowd should be seated on the ground (at the feeding of the 5,000 near Passover in the spring, they sat on green grass [Mark 6:39]; now several months into the dry season, the grass had long since dried up).

After Jesus gave thanks in prayer for the loaves, He began giving[4] them to the disciples for distribution. This is as close as Mark comes to describing the miracle. Jesus just kept giving out the loaves to the disciples, long after the original seven pieces were gone. Likewise with the fish, Jesus asked the Father's blessing upon them in a separate prayer, and then distributed them as He had done with the loaves.

At the conclusion of the meal, seven baskets of food fragments were collected (v. 8). The Greek word for "baskets" used here denotes hampers (larger than the knapsacks used at the feeding of the 5,000); thus the leftovers may have exceeded the twelve knapsacks of the former occasion. The same term for "basket" was used for the large basket in which Paul was lowered through the wall at Damascus (Acts 9:25).

The total who were fed was 4,000. The parallel account in Matthew indicates that this total did not include women and children (Matt. 15:38).

---

[3]Lenski, R. C. H., *The Interpretation of St. Mark's Gospel* (Columbus: Wartburg Press, 1946), 315.
[4]The Greek tense of the verb is the imperfect, which depicts continuing action.

## The Pharisees Demand a Sign, 8:10–12

When the crowd had been fed, Jesus sent them away and then departed with the Twelve by boat to the western side of the Sea of Galilee. Mention of "the boat" (v. 10) implies that this was the boat they had used to come to this particular spot, although nothing has been said in the context about it. One might have assumed that they had come on land with the multitude, since they were already in Decapolis. However, it is possible they used a boat to sail from the site of the healing of the deaf and dumb man to this spot near the shore for the feeding of the 4,000. Another possibility is that this was the boat they customarily used, but it had been left at Capernaum before they began the northward trip to Phoenicia and then to Decapolis. Perhaps friends brought it to the eastern shore when they heard Jesus was working there.[5]

Mark locates the landing at Dalmanutha, which must have been on the west side of the lake. The site is not otherwise known at present. Matthew calls it Magadan (Matt. 15:39).

Upon disembarking at Dalmanutha, Jesus was soon met by some Pharisees (Matthew adds that Sadducees were there also, Matt. 16:1), who demanded that He give them some overpowering proof of His claims. They were not asking for another miracle but for some authentication of His authority to do the miracles. The Mosaic Law required that any miracle-worker who used miracles to lead people away from God should be put to death (Deut. 13:1–5). Mark says they were "testing Him." They were acting in unbelief and even if He had done so, they would doubtless have attributed the power to Beelzebub (Mark 3:22). Perhaps they wanted

---

[5]Hiebert, D. Edmond, *Mark* (Chicago: Moody Press, 1974), 194.

something like Elijah and the fire from heaven that burned up the water-soaked sacrifice (1 Kings 18:30–40).

The failure of the Jewish religious leaders to recognize the presence of God's Messiah in their midst caused Jesus to begin "sighing deeply in His Spirit" (v. 12). Using the form of a Hebrew oath, He said, "[May God smite me] if a sign shall be given to this generation." The meaning was, "No sign shall be given" of the sort they were looking for. Most English versions properly convey the meaning in this fashion (NASB, NIV, KJV).

## A Warning to the Disciples, 8:13–21

The visit to Dalmanutha was a short one, perhaps because of the hostile confrontation with the Pharisees from the beginning, and Jesus embarked with the Twelve to cross the Sea of Galilee once again. This time they went from Dalmanutha to Bethsaida Julias on the northeast side of the lake in Decapolis (v. 22).

While they were sailing across the lake, they realized they had forgotten to take any fresh bread with them. All they had was one loaf that was left from their recent trip. Perhaps their rather abrupt departure caused them to forget these supplies. Apparently they were thinking about this oversight when Jesus began to speak.

"Beware of the leaven of the Pharisees and the leaven of Herod" (v. 15). Jesus was obviously referring to leaven in a symbolic way, intending to picture the permeating but unnoticed effect of the Pharisees' teaching (see Matt. 16:12). In all New Testament uses of leaven as a symbol, it depicts an evil influence, with the possible exception being the Parable of the Leaven (and even this usage may describe the presence of false teaching in the present-day form of the kingdom on earth). In the Markan context, the leaven of the Pharisees would seem to be a reference to their emphasis on conformity to tradition and ritual (Mark 7:1–5), as well as their insistence upon an authenticating sign from heaven (Mark 8:11), which was merely a hypocritical cover for their unbelief (Luke 12:1).

The leaven of Herod is matched in Matthew's parallel account by the mention of Sadducees instead of Herod. These are not really contradictory, however, because the Sadducees controlled the priesthood in Israel and were dependent upon the Herodian rulers to keep them in power. The leavening effect here was doubtless the infiltration of secular interests into one's religious life. Dalmanutha (or Magadan, Magdala) was near Tiberias, the capital of Galilee under Herod Antipas, and that could have prompted this particular reference.

The disciples, however, misinterpreted Jesus' statement about leaven and supposed He was rebuking them for forgetting the provisions for the trip. Jesus knew what they were thinking and questioned why they were so slow in understanding the bigger picture. Could it be they were just momentarily forgetful, or were their hearts actually hardened and impervious to His person and His teaching? The answer was probably a bit of both. Jesus then quoted two Old Testament passages that described Israel as unable to use the eyes and ears they possessed (Jer. 5:21; Ezek. 12:2).

To answer the disciples' obsessive concern about food, Jesus reminded them of the two recent incidents of His miraculous feeding of huge crowds, and asked how many containers of fragments they picked up. Their memory of the facts was excellent, but they did not seem to have learned the lesson. It is of interest to note that Jesus carefully restricted

His use of "baskets"[6] to the earlier episode of the 5,000, and "large baskets"[7] to the feeding of the 4,000. As indicated earlier, the seven large baskets (hampers) of fragments may have contained more than the twelve baskets (knapsacks, picnic baskets) of the first feeding.

Jesus emphasized in His questioning the quantity of fragments left over from the feeding to show that He was also concerned about meeting the needs of the Twelve. If He had clearly met their needs on two recent occasions, surely they could trust Him to care for them again, even if He had to take that one remaining loaf and multiply it! Then Jesus asked them again, "Do you not yet understand?" (v. 21). Matthew indicates that only then did they understand what He was saying (Matt. 16:12).

## Healing of a Blind Man at Bethsaida, 8:22–26

This miracle and the healing of the deaf mute in 7:31–37 are recorded only by Mark.

Jesus and the Twelve crossed the sea and landed in Gaulanitis near Bethsaida Julias, avoiding Galilee, which was ruled by Herod Antipas (see discussion on Mark 6:14–29). Bethsaida had recently been enlarged and given the status of a city by Herod Philip, tetrarch of Gaulanitis, who named it in honor of Caesar Augustus' daughter Julia.[8] Mark still calls it a village, using the older but more common name.

A blind man was brought to Jesus, who then took him outside the village to a more private place where they would not be disturbed. That this miracle was performed in stages

---

[6]Greek: *kophinos*
[7]Greek: *spuris*
[8]Josephus, *Antiquities of the Jews*, 18.28.

does not imply that Jesus was having difficulty with the miracle, for someone who can raise the dead has all the power He needs to heal (Mark 5:35–43). It should also be remembered that all stages of this miracle were accomplished within minutes of each other, so it was not a long, drawn-out process. The purpose for this unusual procedure is not explained, but perhaps it was done to assist the man in recognizing one step at a time what was happening to him.

At the first stage of healing the man reported, he could see men walking about and they looked to him like trees (v. 24). This may imply that the man had not been born blind; otherwise, he would not have recognized trees as trees. At the second stage the man saw everything clearly. The miracle was complete and perfect. Then Jesus sent the man home. He was not to go back into the village where the excitable populace might demand more miracles and prevent Jesus from concentrating on teaching ministry.

## Peter's Confession of Jesus as the Christ, 8:27–30

Caesarea Philippi is about twenty-five miles north of Bethsaida, and was the residence of Herod Philip. It is located at the foot of Mount Hermon, and gushing springs there form one of the sources of the Jordan River. Mark and Matthew both say that Jesus came to the villages or district of Caesarea Philippi, but do not indicate that He actually went to the city itself. This would seem to be consistent with His purpose of avoiding crowds at this time in order to devote Himself to the instruction of the Twelve.

As Jesus and the Twelve were on the way toward Caesarea Philippi, He asked them what the people were saying as to His identity (v. 27). They responded with several

Fig. 9. Banias, site of Caesarea Philippi, on slopes of Mount Hermon. Springs emerging from the cave in center come from the snows on Mount Hermon and form one of the sources of the Jordan River.

suggestions that were circulating. One was John the Baptist, the same notion that had been adopted by Herod Antipas (Mark 6:14–16). Another identification made by some was the resurrected Elijah, based in part on Malachi 4:5. Others simply suggested that one of the early prophets had risen from the dead. All of these views reflect a Jewish belief in bodily resurrection, even though they were mistaken in identifying Jesus in such a way.

Then Jesus asked the Twelve directly, "But who do you say that I am?" (v. 29). Knowing that most of the general population had inadequate ideas about the Messiah, He wanted the Twelve to verbalize their own understanding. Peter, perhaps acting in his usual capacity as the spokesman for the group, said, "Thou art the Christ." Mark's account is the briefest of the three parallels (see Matt. 16:16; Luke

9:20), perhaps because it was based on Peter's preaching, which did not wish to unduly magnify his understanding. Of course, the Twelve had acknowledged He was the Messiah much earlier in their following of Him (John 1:40–51), but now it was important for them to confirm that understanding in light of false or inadequate opinions in circulation.

The Twelve were then cautioned not to tell anyone about Him (v. 30). Matthew makes it clear that it was the identity of Jesus as Messiah that was not to be circulated by them (16:20). This was almost certainly because the general populace thought solely in terms of a political or military deliverer, without giving any heed to the Old Testament teaching of the Suffering Servant who would die for their sins as the Lamb of God (Isa. 53; see also John 1:29). Spreading the word of Jesus as Messiah ran the risk of fueling the fires of insurrection, which Jesus did not wish to do.

## First Prediction of Jesus' Death and Resurrection, 8:31–38

"Began to teach them" (v. 31) probably means more than just "to tell them." It suggests some discussion, giving of reasons, and making an effort to be sure the instruction was learned. In this instance, Jesus was teaching the Twelve some very hard things which they found exceedingly difficult to accept. He explained that He would be rejected by the religious leadership of the nation and would be killed.[9] Previously Jesus had given some general, more-veiled statements to this effect, but now He told them plainly (see Mark 2:20 for an example). He also added the fact that He would rise

---

[9]This is the first of three predictions given by Jesus regarding His coming death and resurrection that Mark records. The others are given in 9:30–32 and 10:32–34.

again, not just in the resurrection that was promised to all the righteous but "after three days." The phrase in Matthew and Luke is recorded as "on the third day," indicating that these phrases meant the same thing in Jewish terminology (Matt. 16:21; Luke 9:22). Similar imprecision is common in English as well.[10]

Peter did not appreciate the statement of Jesus at all, and took Jesus aside to rebuke Him. Jesus, however, using the same verb, rebuked Peter. To some extent Peter must have shared the popular opinion of a conquering Messiah, and Jesus needed to correct him. Before doing so, He looked at the rest of the disciples and included them as witnesses of His statement, probably because He knew they shared Peter's feelings.

Addressing Peter, He said, "Get behind Me, Satan" (v. 33). Jesus understood that Satan had influenced Peter's thinking at this point, for Satan had used the same tactics on Jesus in the wilderness temptation when he offered Jesus the kingdom without the need for suffering (Matt. 4:8–10). Of course, Jesus did not mean that Peter was demon-possessed, for He performed no act of exorcism, but He did mean that Peter was being influenced by Satan with this kind of thinking. Peter's problem was that he was allowing mere human goals and procedures to take the place of God's program. Doubtless this incident was in Peter's mind when he wrote in his epistle, "Your adversary, the devil, prowls about like a roaring lion, seeking someone to devour" (1 Peter 5:8).

At this point Jesus summoned the crowd that must have been following throughout the previous episode, and had heard some of His discussion with the Twelve. To them He

---

[10]When we say we will do something "in three days," it is not always clear whether we are counting the present as day one and thus the third day would actually be two days from now, or whether a full seventy-two hours is meant.

said that anyone who wished to enlist as one of His followers needed to be prepared for two things. First, he needed to "deny himself" (v. 34). This was not talking about some temporary self-denial of luxuries or pleasures, but a denial of one's self. One's plans, goals, interests, and motives must be abandoned, and everything must be centered on the Lord Jesus Christ whom we would follow. This is what it means to become a disciple or follower of Christ.

The second thing a would-be follower of Jesus must be prepared for is to "take up his cross." To any first-century resident of Palestine, crucifixion was a well-known form of Roman execution. The hearers would have understood Jesus to mean that becoming a follower of Him involved the recognition that He was going to His death, and His followers were risking the same. Jesus did not want to enlist followers under false pretenses. His cause was going to bring death to Him and possibly the same for His followers.

The paradoxical statement of verse 35 turns upon the wide use of the term "life" (Greek: *psuche*). It refers to that element which animates the body, but it also denotes that element in which the consciousness and spirit reside and which lives on after death. "Life" and "soul" are two English attempts to translate the various aspects of this many-sided word. The point of Jesus seems to be that the person who seeks to save his life during persecution by denying Christ will eventually lose it forever (in its eternal aspects). On the other hand, the person who loses his life because of devotion to Christ will find that he has really preserved it eternally. Jesus then summarized His remarks by noting the folly of trading away the eternal salvation of the soul for the temporary gains of life in this world. Once the eternal soul is lost, what could possibly be used to buy it back? (vv. 36–37).

Jesus then raised the discussion to the great consummation of God's program when He as the Son of Man will return to earth in glory (v. 38). Calling Himself the Son of Man is surely a reflection of Daniel 7:13–14, which describes the establishment of God's kingdom on earth. At that time, said Jesus, those who have failed to acknowledge Him will not be acknowledged by Him. Thus the awesome significance of a genuine commitment to Him is clearly set forth.

## Truths to Remember

• When Jesus fed the 4,000, He did it out of compassion for their needs not as a strategy to impress or entertain the crowd.

• When Christ does His works among men, He may use a variety of methods.

• Christ's expectations of His followers are demanding and serious.

# 9

## EXCURSIONS AROUND AND OUTSIDE GALILEE – III
### Mark 9:1–50

### The Transfiguration, 9:1–13

The event we call the Transfiguration was surely one of the most dramatic in the career of Jesus, and yet it is one of the least understood. Perhaps this is partly because it is difficult for us to see in the Transfiguration any immediate relevance to Christ's redemptive work. The birth, baptism, temptation, crucifixion, resurrection, and ascension of Jesus all have some clearly indicated bearing on His mission, but this is not so readily seen regarding the Transfiguration. Nevertheless, the event was important enough to be entitled to a place in all three Synoptic Gospels.

Less than one year remained until the Crucifixion. The Transfiguration occurred during the time when Jesus was withdrawing as much as possible from the crowds in Galilee in order to find opportunity to instruct the disciples. He made four such withdrawals, beginning at Passover season in A.D. 29. The first was to the eastern shore of Galilee, during which time He fed the 5,000 (Mark 6:30–44). The second withdrawal was to the northwest, the region of Tyre and Sidon, where He healed the daughter of the Syrophoenician woman (Mark 7:24–30). The third one took Him into

Decapolis (Mark 7:31). On the fourth withdrawal Jesus took His disciples northeast of the Sea of Galilee to the region of Caesarea Philippi (Mark 8:27). It was at this time that the Transfiguration occurred.

Although there had been many indications that Jesus was at the height of His popularity with the people, He had recently told His disciples He was going to be killed in Jerusalem (Matt. 16:21, Mark 8:31). Even though He also told them He would rise again, the prospect of His death was most distressing to the disciples.

### The Prediction, 9:1

When Jesus foretold His coming rejection, death, and resurrection, the disciples became greatly unnerved. Satan actually prompted Peter to rebuke Jesus and attempt to dissuade Him from His announced plan (Mark 8:31–33). As an encouragement to His disciples Jesus announced that some of them would not die without seeing the kingdom of God. Matthew says that the prediction involved seeing "the Son of man coming in his kingdom" (Matt. 16:28). Mark records the prediction as seeing "the kingdom of God after it has come with power."

This passage is sometimes used by those who do not believe Christ will return to establish a literal kingdom. Since none of the Twelve lived to see the Second Coming, the critics explain that what is meant in verse 1 is a prediction of His coming in judgment on Jerusalem in A.D. 70, at which time the city was destroyed. However, it is noteworthy that all three Synoptic Gospels place this prediction immediately before the Transfiguration (Matt. 16:28, Luke 9:27). Furthermore, Mark's Gospel, which may have been based on Peter's recollections,[1] contains the words "with power" in connection with the coming of the kingdom. It seems significant that Peter uses the same word "power" in connection with the coming of the kingdom to describe the Transfiguration:

> For we did not follow cleverly devised tales, when we made known to you the *power* and *coming of our Lord Jesus Christ,* but we were eyewitnesses of his majesty. For when He received honor and glory from God the Father, such an utterance as this was made to Him by the Majestic Glory, "This is my beloved Son with whom I am well pleased"—and we ourselves heard this utterance made from heaven when we were with Him on *the holy mountain* (2 Peter 1:16–18, emphasis added).

Thus Peter, who was one of the three who witnessed the event, realized he had received a foretaste of the coming of Christ in power when he saw the Transfiguration.

## The Setting, 9:2a

Six days after the preceding prediction, Jesus took three of His disciples to a high mountain. Luke says it was "some eight days" (9:28). Rather than imagining a discrepancy, the difference may be explained by understanding Mark (and Matthew) to have referred only to the interval of six days, while Luke counts both termini (the day of the prediction and the day of the Transfiguration).

This was the second of three instances in which Peter, James, and John were granted special privileges (the first was

[1]See Chapter 1, "Authorship of the Gospel," 2–3.

at the raising of Jairus' daughter, Mark 5:37). No explanation is offered in Scripture as to why these three were selected. Perhaps they had the greatest spiritual discernment among the Twelve at this time and would be able to appreciate more readily what would transpire. Certainly they were outstanding among the Twelve. In all our lists of the apostles, their names appear among the first four mentioned.

The high mountain to which they went has been traditionally identified as Mount Tabor in the Jezreel Valley in Galilee. A Franciscan church on the summit commemorates the event. However, both Matthew (16:13) and Mark (8:27) mention Jesus as being in the region of Caesarea Philippi, and Mount Tabor is much too far away. More likely the Transfiguration occurred on one of the spurs of Mount Hermon, which towers above Caesarea Philippi.

Fig. 10. Mount Hermon (elev. 9,200 ft.), the most probable location of the Transfiguration.

**The Transformation, 9:2b–3**

This event probably took place at night, which would explain why the disciples slept. Also, Jesus had gone with these disciples in order to find seclusion for prayer, a practice He commonly followed at night (Luke 9:28). Furthermore, when they came down from the mountain, it was said to be the "next day" (Luke 9:37). With the darkness of night as the setting, the dazzling nature of the Transfiguration would be all the more striking.

Suddenly Jesus' appearance underwent a dramatic change. Mark described it as a glistening whiteness, not only of His physical body but also of His garments. Christ's appearance was superior to anything possible on earth. Matthew described it as a brightness like the sun (Matt. 17:2). The word that has been translated "transfigured"[2] in our English Bibles occurs four times in the New Testament. Two of the instances refer to the Transfiguration. The other uses are in Romans 12:2 and 2 Corinthians 3:18 (translated as "transformed"). The basic idea of the word is a change of form brought about by what is inherent, rather than some external form that is put on. From the same Greek word has come our word "metamorphosis," to describe an inherent transformation like that of a caterpillar into a butterfly.

What happened to Jesus was a transformation from within in which His essential glory was revealed to the eyes of His apostles. Ordinarily this was veiled during Christ's earthly ministry. Because He had spoken of His coming death, the disciples needed some encouragement. It was provided by this dramatic revelation of the glory of Christ that everyone will see when His Kingdom is actually established on the

---

[2]Greek: *metamorphoō*

earth. If their attention was focused on the glory to come, they would be able to survive their coming trials.

### The Visitors, 9:4

In the midst of this impressive scene Elijah and Moses appeared and engaged in conversation with Jesus. These two, who had passed from the earthly scene many centuries before, still possessed life and consciousness. Why were these particular individuals from the Old Testament present on the mount? They may have been there as representatives. Moses the lawgiver epitomized the whole Old Testament period which was characterized by the law. Paul later wrote that the Law was "our tutor to lead us to Christ" (Gal. 3: 24). In view of their conversation and of what the voice from heaven said, Moses' presence seems to have shown to the disciples that in Jesus the shadows of the Law were all fulfilled and now withdrawn. Elijah was the most representative of all the prophets who might have been selected. Although the average Christian probably would have selected one of the writing prophets, such as Isaiah, because of their predictions of Christ, to the Jews of Jesus' day it was Elijah who exemplified the office of prophet most perfectly.

Mark does not mention the topic of conversation, but Luke tells us that Jesus, Moses, and Elijah discussed the approaching death of Jesus at Jerusalem (Luke 9:30–31). This would have demonstrated to the disciples that Christ's death, which was so difficult for them to accept, must have been compatible with the Old Testament, for these Old Testament saints could discuss it with Jesus without any apparent disagreement.

### The Suggestion from Peter, 9:5–6

Peter responded to the situation ("answered" does not necessarily mean he had been addressed) by suggesting that three shelter booths be constructed for the distinguished visitors and Jesus. According to Matthew, Peter volunteered to build them (Matt. 17:4). Did he assume the kingdom had now arrived and these visitors would need earthly provision? Or, was he merely gracious, suggesting that this conference be prolonged? Perhaps we should not look too hard for a logical explanation of his words, since Mark tells us the comment was not well thought out. All of the disciples had become terrified in the presence of the supernatural, and thus Peter's response was more emotional than reasonable.

The implication of his words seems to be that he desired to learn more from each of these men. Seeing Moses and Elijah, these greatly revered figures from Jewish history, made Peter forget that just a week before he had made a confession that lifted Christ completely out of the realm of other men (Matt. 16:16).

### The Answer, 9:7–8

Before Jesus or the two Old Testament men could answer, a cloud enveloped the group, thus hampering normal communication. Then came the voice of God from heaven, heard out of the cloud: "This is my beloved Son: Listen to Him." This message from God made it very clear that Jesus was unique. He was God's Son, in that special sense enjoyed by no one else.

Furthermore, the command "Listen to Him" stressed that the ministries of Moses and Elijah were finished. They had spoken the message of God in their day, but that day was now past. It was not appropriate to have three tabernacles so that all three might be listened to equally. Now God has spoken to us in His Son, and He is above all other revealers of God's truth (Heb. 1:2).

This truth was conveyed not only by the Father's voice, but also by the events that followed. Elijah and Moses disappeared, and only Jesus was left. Thus, by historical event as well as by voice, the truth of Christ's uniqueness and superiority was emphasized.

### The Subsequent Discussion, 9:9–13

*Regarding the Resurrection of Christ, 9:9–10.* As the little group made its way down from the mountain, Jesus told them not to tell anyone what they had seen until after the Resurrection. Apparently they were not even to inform the other nine disciples. Perhaps this was because the people in general, and even some of the Twelve, had many erroneous ideas about what messiahship meant. To speak of what they had just witnessed to those whose chief concern was for a political leader might only confuse and perhaps politically excite the less perceptive. After the Resurrection there would not be the same danger of a popular uprising, because Jesus would no longer be with men in the same way.

Jesus had previously told them of His coming death and resurrection after three days (Mark 8:31). Yet, the actual fact did not seem to register with them. Because they did not want to believe, they refused to believe and then complained that they did not understand.

*Regarding Elijah, 9:11–13.* The disciples then raised a question about Elijah. They mentioned it was a common rabbinical teaching, based on Malachi 4:5–6, that Elijah would return to earth prior to Messiah's coming. Since they had just seen Elijah on the mount, they may have wondered whether that prophecy had just been fulfilled and whether the kingdom of Messiah could now be inaugurated. They may also have been puzzled about the necessity of Christ's death in view of the fact that Elijah had just appeared and the establishment of the kingdom seemed to be very near. Jesus answered, "Elijah does first come." He confirmed the basic truth of the scribes' interpretation of Malachi 4:5–6. He also reminded them of other prophecies that foretold the sufferings of the Messiah. These had been predicted in Scripture even more frequently than the coming of Elijah (see Isaiah 53). Thus, it must occur, and the presence of Elijah on the mount did not rule out the need for Christ to suffer.

He went on to say, however, that in a sense Elijah had come already (see Matt. 17:12). Because of His explanation that the people had already done to Elijah what they desired, it is obvious Jesus was not referring to the Elijah who had just appeared on the mount, but to some prior person. The parallel passage in Matthew makes it clear that He was referring to John the Baptist (Matt. 17:13), who had been executed. He did not mean that John was the Old Testament prophet reincarnated, but that he had performed an Elijah-like work in preparing the hearts of the nation for the Messiah's coming (Luke 1:17). John the Baptist himself denied he was Elijah in person (John 1:21). But he had been mistreated, just as Elijah was at the hand of Ahab and Jezebel ("just as it is written of him"; see 1 Kings 19:1–3). Because of John's ministry, which was in the "spirit and power of Elijah" (Luke 1:17), Israel should have responded in faith and thus have been ready to receive Jesus as Messiah.

As this remarkable experience drew to its close, we can see more clearly how it did provide a foretaste of the coming messianic kingdom. L. S. Chafer in his *Systematic Theology*[3] points out that the Transfiguration provided all the essential elements of the messianic kingdom. The glorified Christ was there as the central figure. Glorified saints were there, represented by Moses and Elijah. And Jews still on earth but enjoying the kingdom are represented by the three disciples.

## Healing of a Mute Boy with an Evil Spirit, 9:14–29

All three Gospels that record the Transfiguration also record this miracle as the next event. Luke explains more precisely that it was the next day (Luke 9:37). It provided a visual reminder that the glories of the messianic kingdom to come must not make us unaware of present problems or of our complete dependence upon God's power to meet those problems.

### The Problem, 9:14–24

As Jesus and the three disciples came back to the other nine who had been left behind, they saw a large crowd surrounding them. A discussion was in progress between them and some scribes. When they saw Jesus, they were surprised and ran to Him. His arrival was unexpected but certainly opportune. Their being "amazed" (v. 15) should not be understood as meaning that Jesus' face still retained some of the radiance from the Transfiguration (as, for example, Moses' face when he came from Sinai, Ex. 34:29–30), for Mark gives no hint of that. Their amazement was more likely their surprise at Christ's arrival at this particular moment.

[3]L. S. Chafer, *Systematic Theology* (Dallas: Dallas Seminary Press, 1948), VII, 305–306.

Jesus asked the scribes what they were discussing with the nine disciples. A man from the crowd explained that he had brought his child, who had frequent convulsions induced by an evil spirit, to Jesus for help. Unable to find Jesus, he had appealed to the nine disciples, who had been unsuccessful in curing him. Perhaps the scribes had been arguing that their methods were wrong, because some of the Jews claimed the power of casting out demons (see Luke 11:19). All of this must have been most embarrassing to the disciples.

Jesus' reply was apparently directed to the entire multitude, whose faithlessness was demonstrated by the scribal opposition to His disciples. When He called for the lad to be brought, the evil spirit caused another seizure. The father explained that this condition had been occurring since early childhood, with much danger to the child's life. The father's faith was very weak ("if You can do anything," v. 22), but at least he turned to Jesus for aid.

The response of Jesus (v. 23) picked up the words of the father. He explained, "As for your statement, 'If you can do anything,' the answer is that there is nothing deficient in My faith, and therefore it is certain that I can perform the will of God in this matter." This comment would also cause the man to examine his own faith. The father did precisely this and reacted with the cry that in some sense expresses the feeling of all believers at various times: "I do believe; help my unbelief" (v. 24).

### The Miracle, 9:25–29

Jesus then commanded the demon to leave the boy. The evil spirit obeyed immediately, but the lad experienced a final convulsion in the process. When it was over and the demon was gone, the exhausted lad was limp and apparently lifeless. Jesus then touched his hand, and he received strength to stand. This was one of a very few miracles that occurred in two stages. (The healing of the blind man at Bethsaida was another, Mark 8:22–26).

Somewhat later, when the group of disciples got away from the crowd at the foot of the mountain and entered a house, the nine asked Jesus privately about their failure. The inference is that they had tried and failed. When Jesus answered, His words "this kind" imply that there are different kinds of demons and the one in question was more difficult to cast out than others. This demon, He said, could come out only "by prayer." Only an appeal to the direct power of God would be able to overcome this sort of satanic power. Apparently the nine had not prayed, and perhaps had looked to their own powers or to some formula as a magical source. They needed to trust God directly and show that trust through prayer. ("And fasting" is not found in our two oldest and most reliable manuscripts and should be omitted.)

## Second Prediction of Jesus' Death and Resurrection, 9:30–32

Jesus and the Twelve now returned to Galilee and eventually arrived in Capernaum (9:33). He had been with them outside of Galilee in order to focus on teaching them away from the huge crowds. Having returned to Galilee, He still was attempting to maintain some privacy while conveying some very crucial information.

Jesus gave a second prediction[4] of His coming death and resurrection, repeating His announcement given in 8:31.

[4]The first prediction is recorded in Mark 8:31–38 and the third in 10:32–34.

132

This time, however, He added that He would be betrayed ("delivered") into the hands of men (v. 31). They had been so shocked and unaccepting of His previous announcement of coming death that Jesus did not at that time give the additional information of betrayal. They needed to be informed in stages.

Unfortunately, they still did not comprehend, though why is not clear. Luke indicates that the full import was concealed from them but does not explain why (Luke 9:45). Matthew says they were deeply grieved (Matt. 17:23), and Mark and Luke say they were afraid to ask Jesus about it (Luke 9:45). Sometimes people prefer not to have dire prospects spelled out, simply because they do not wish to think about them.

## A Dispute among the Disciples, 9:33–37

On this itineration in Galilee, Jesus and the Twelve came to Capernaum and went into "the house" (v. 33). This was probably the house in Capernaum that was mentioned earlier (v. 28). Whether it was the house of Peter or the house to which Jesus had moved His family cannot be ascertained. Here Jesus began to question them about their conversation on the road. Apparently they had been walking with Jesus at the head of a single file, as was common for itinerant teachers and disciples. Jesus had not been part of their conversation, although He knew what they had been saying (Luke 9:47) and wanted them to own up to it.

The Twelve, however, were too embarrassed to confess that they had been arguing about their relative positions in Christ's program and particularly His coming kingdom. Perhaps the special privilege given to Peter, James, and John at the Transfiguration had prompted this discussion. Their arguing also implies they were placing too much emphasis on the external glories of the kingdom, just as the general populace regularly did. This would have made Christ's announcement of His death most difficult to understand (v. 32).

Jesus, therefore, called the Twelve around Him and showed He knew exactly what their argument had been about. He explained that being "first" in His view demands being "last" and acting like a "servant" (v. 35). The all-too-human jockeying for position is not God's way. He illustrated His point by taking a child and setting him before the disciples. The child may have lived in the home; perhaps he was a child of one of the disciples. We may assume, from his lack of timidity, that he may have known Jesus. Then Jesus took the child in His arms and said that humbly accommodating oneself to the needs of a child, rather than striving to get ahead of other adults, displays the attitude Christ wants, and is a way of receiving Christ Himself and His message. Even more, such an action is pleasing to God, for it is He who has sent Christ (v. 37).

## John's Mistaken Zeal, 9:38–50

The setting here seems to be the same as the previous incident, for no change of any kind is indicated. John brought up a circumstance that had bothered him and the others. They had come in contact with someone who was casting out demons in the name of Jesus, and yet that person was not a part of their group. That person must have been so impressed with Jesus and His power that he began to use it in his own performance. The Twelve tried to stop him, out of loyalty to Jesus, no doubt, but now they seemed to be having second thoughts.

Jesus, however, told the Twelve to let the man alone (v. 39). He explained that anyone who was successfully using His name to perform miracles would hardly be one who in the next breath spoke evil of Him. If the man's actions were not against Jesus and His immediate followers, he should be regarded not as a rival but as a friend (v. 40). Intolerance of other friends of Christ must be avoided.[5] Anyone who offers help to believers because they are believers ("because of your name as followers of Christ") will be acknowledged by Christ and properly rewarded. Even the smallest service done for Christ ("a cup of water") will not go unnoticed by Him, because what is done for His servants He regards as being done for Him (v. 41, compare v. 37).

On the other hand, mistreatment of "one of these little ones who believe" (v. 42) is a most serious offense. This seems to refer to childlike believers rather than simply babies or children (see the parallel in Matt. 18:1–14). Such mistreatment of believers, even those who might be regarded as small and insignificant, merits extreme punishment. Tying a heavy millstone (the kind requiring a donkey to move, rather than the smaller hand mill sort) around the neck and then being thrown into the sea is a graphic metaphor. Present-day visitors to ancient Capernaum can see a display of such millstones in a garden along the seashore, making the words of Jesus most graphic.

---

[5]A similar statement by Jesus is recorded in Matthew 12:30, which at first glance seems contradictory: "He who is not with Me is against Me." However, in that instance Jesus was talking about those who were clearly opposed to Him, and this opposition needed to be recognized. In the Mark instance above, He was talking about sympathizers with His ministry.

Verses 43, 45, and 47 emphasize the need for His followers to do whatever it takes to avoid causing spiritual harm to other believers. The repetition of the same advice, but using the hand, the foot, and the eye as examples, reminded the hearers they needed to be alert to whatever sort of activity they were involved in that might cause others to stumble. The hand, foot, and eye are the chief members of the body employed in human activity and thus provide apt metaphors. Ultimately, of course, Jesus did not mean this literally, for sin is basically a spiritual problem of the heart, not the physical misuse of hands, feet, or eyes. Nevertheless, the analogy is good, for surgeons do not hesitate to amputate a limb if disease threatens the life of the body. Likewise, in the spiritual realm, when the choice lies between a sacrifice of something in this life or an eternity in the unquenchable fires of hell,[6] the decision should not be too difficult to make.

Verses 44 and 46 do not appear in the most reliable ancient manuscripts, and thus are put in brackets in NASB and as footnotes in NIV. The words were obviously added by copyists from verse 48, where they properly belong. They are taken from Isaiah 66:24 and serve to describe in graphic terms the eternal punishment of the wicked.

"For everyone will be salted with fire" (v. 49) is a most difficult statement to fit into the previous context without violating the sense of what follows. Variant readings in the manuscripts point out this difficulty, but the text adopted above is found in most English translations today and has the best manuscript support. The background may lie in

---

[6]Greek: *geennan*. The term was derived from the Valley of Hinnom on the west of Jerusalem, which served as the city dump, with its smoldering fires, and was once the scene of human sacrifices.

Leviticus 2:13, where all of the grain offerings that were to be burned upon the altar must first have salt applied. The next verse in Mark will explain the importance of believers having "salt" in their lives. In verse 49, however, believers (and especially the Twelve) must recognize that as followers of Jesus they should expect some fiery trials as well because they were sacrificing themselves (cf. 1 Peter 4:12–14). To be "salted with fire" points to this prospect.

Verse 50 explains that "salt is good." Its chief function in the ancient world was as a preservative to keep food pure, and also as a seasoning and flavor enhancer. These characteristics should be present in the lives of believers. They should be pure in their own lives, and be promoters of purity in their contacts with others. "If the salt becomes unsalty" refers to something that often happened in the ancient world. Pure salt does not deteriorate in our modern containers, but salt obtained from the Dead Sea and from mines was often impure. The salt could leach out because of too much moisture, and what was left was gypsum or other minerals. Such "salt" was useless. It offered no protection against food spoilage, and certainly did not make the flavor better.

"Have salt in yourselves and be at peace with one another" (v. 50b). Salt was also used in the ratifying of covenants (Lev. 2:13b; Num. 18:19). Perhaps that feature is reflected in the comment to be at peace with one another. Being at peace means that there are no broken relationships. When the believer's life is characterized by having "salt," it implies he is living a pure life, he is promoting purity among others, and he is keeping his relationships with others in good order.

## Truths to Remember

• The transformation Christ experienced on the mount is also to be experienced by believers. During this life, a gradual change occurs as we become more Christlike (2 Cor. 3:18), but it will be complete when we see Him in glory (1 John 3:2).

• Christ is the highest revelation of God and is to be listened to above all others.

• All service that pleases God must look to Him for power.

• Other believers, even if they are not part of one's group, are to be recognized and supported as fellow members of Christ's body.

# Part II

## The Ministry on the Way to Jerusalem

### Mark 10:1–52

# 10

# THE FINAL JOURNEY TO JERUSALEM
## Mark 10:1–52

The Transfiguration (Mark 9) was a turning point in the career of Jesus. From that point on, the Gospel writers indicate repeatedly that His face was set toward Jerusalem. Luke, after reporting the Transfiguration in 9:27–36, states in verse 51, "He resolutely set his face to go to Jerusalem." Mark 10:32 says, "They were in the road, going up to Jerusalem." This new emphasis in our Lord's ministry is also seen in how He now spoke repeatedly and more precisely about His coming death. Jesus had given veiled hints of His death from the earliest days of His ministry (John 2:19–22). Beginning with the Transfiguration (actually it began about a week before, Mark 8:31–9:2), Jesus foretold explicitly His coming rejection, death, and resurrection.

Consequently, His actions as He led His disciples during these days are especially thought provoking. What He said and what He did were the things He wanted to accomplish when He knew His time on earth was running out. Because He knew what would soon take place, we must understand that He chose carefully many of the topics for discussion and used the situations that occurred as opportunities to convey His teachings to His disciples.

Traveling with Jesus during these days must have been a fascinating experience. He attracted all types of people with the widest range of problems. Yet He never thought it necessary to wall Himself off from men. The unique way in which Jesus dealt with personal problems made His ministry remarkable. He was never tedious and dull. His method was direct and incisive. His answers were never tentative or apologetic.

## Teaching about Divorce, 10:1–12

### The Setting, 10:1

In Mark's account, the journey began "from there," and this locates Jesus in Capernaum and its environs (9:33). However, Mark goes on to describe the events "beyond the Jordan" (that is, the province of Perea) that brought Jesus to Jerusalem for the final time. However, he makes no mention of some extensive travel before that final trip. Between the time of the Transfiguration, which occurred in the late summer, and the final trip to Jerusalem, which culminated in the Crucifixion at the next Passover in the spring, there were about six months that Mark does not describe but that are mentioned elsewhere. Mark omits the material included in John 7:1–11:54 and Luke 9:51–18:34, which describes a trip to Jerusalem for the feast of tabernacles in October (John 7:2–14), a ministry in various parts of Judea, a return to Jerusalem for the feast of dedication in December (John 10:22–23), a ministry in Perea (John 10:40–42), a return to Bethany in Judea for the raising of Lazarus (John 11), and then a trip north through Samaria to Galilee where He may have joined the pilgrims who were heading to Jerusalem for the Passover (Luke 17:11).

Mark's statement in verse 1 summarizes Jesus' activity after He left Galilee for the last time. Jesus crossed to the east side of the Jordan River. He then moved south through

Perea until He was opposite the province of Judea but still on the far side of the Jordan River. During this period He was customarily attracting crowds of people and using these occasions for instruction on various subjects.

## The Question, 10:2

It was during such a time that some Pharisees came to Jesus with a question. The Pharisees were the most religiously orthodox of the Jewish groups, but they were also the most frequently denounced by Jesus. Their loud insistence on observing the letter of the Old Testament law was termed hypocrisy by Jesus, because it was not accompanied by spiritual understanding. Theirs was a legalistic system of righteousness by works and was contrary to what God had revealed about the source of true righteousness.

The Pharisees asked whether the Mosaic Law allowed a man to divorce his wife. This age-old issue was much in dispute in Jesus' day. The teaching of an earlier rabbi, Shammai, was very strict as far as many Jews were concerned, for he allowed divorce only in the instance of Deuteronomy 24:1. Another influential rabbi, Hillel, allowed divorce on many grounds. Rabbi Akiba taught that a man could divorce his wife if she failed to please him any longer. Laws on divorce were interpreted in a very lax fashion in Jesus' day.

Mark says that the Pharisees were testing Jesus with their question. They were not really seeking information but trying to provoke an argument in order to find a new way to accuse Him. Perhaps they felt He would deny all divorce (because of His high spiritual standards), and then they could say He was contradicting what Moses taught.

**The Explanation, 10:3–9**

Before giving His answer, Jesus asked a counter question. By sending the Pharisees back to the Mosaic Law, He served notice that He was not an innovator but intended to keep the discussion on biblical ground. This method also forced His questioners to voice the biblical teaching, with which they could hardly disagree.

The Pharisees cited Deuteronomy 24:1, which allowed divorce provided that the husband would give his wife a certificate that stated the charge against her. (Women could not normally obtain divorces in Jewish society.) Jesus explained, however, that this regulation was not God's desire for men; it was not His original intention. It was in a sense a concession to human weakness necessitated by sin, which had intruded after creation. The certificate of divorce was not intended as a provision for men to divorce their wives, but for the protection of wives against capricious and unwarranted actions by unfaithful husbands. Only in cases where the cause ("indecency") was flagrant and clear was divorce to be allowed under Mosaic legislation.

Jesus then went on to show from Genesis, which Moses also wrote, that God's intention in creation was that men and women live in the relation of marriage, not its dissolution (1:27, 5:2). Even before Eve was created, Adam was created as a male. Marriage must therefore have been God's ideal and original intention. Jesus next cited Genesis 2:24, which states that God has created man in such a way that he will forsake his closest social tie—the family in which he was reared—and be joined in marriage to a woman. As a result, there is formed an infinitely closer relationship. Only God's plan and provision can really account for such a phenomenon.

Inasmuch as the marriage union is a joining by God's own plan, whatever disrupts the union (aside from death) is opposed to the will of God (v. 9).

### A Further Explanation, 10:10–12

Somewhat later, when Jesus had gotten away from the crowds and was with His disciples in a house, they questioned Him further on the matter. According to Matthew 19:10, they wondered whether it might not be better to avoid marriage entirely if the divine requirements were this rigid: "If the relationship of the man with his wife is like this, it is better not to marry." This is surely a commentary on the attitude of Jewish society, in which the escape provided by divorce was regarded as a basic necessity.

To the disciples Jesus spoke clearly of God's will regarding marriage. If a man divorces his wife and marries another, he commits adultery against her. It makes no difference that a legal divorce procedure has been carried out. In God's sight the man is still joined to his first wife. The same holds true for a wife who divorces her husband. Although this latter case was not normally possible among the Jews (and Matthew's Gospel does not include it in his account), Jesus was enunciating the general principle, and Mark may have reported it because he was writing for a Roman readership.

Mark's account stresses the basic principle of God's intention for marriage, and that various legal regulations are the unfortunate necessity when God's will has been forsaken. R. T. France expressed it well: "The legal provision of Moses in Deut. 24 was not intended as a statement of God's purpose for marriage, but as a regrettable but necessary means of limiting the damage when that purpose has already been abandoned."[1] He also cautions us:

> But if we are to do justice to Mark's understanding of Jesus, we will do so not by attempting to weaken his bold statement of God's purpose for marriage but by recognizing any broken marriage for what it is, a breach of God's standard, and by regarding any resultant provision for divorce not as good, but as, like the Mosaic legislation in Deut. 24:1–4, a regrettable concession to *sklērokardia* [hardness of heart].[2]

## Teaching about Children, 10:13–16

If this incident occurred in the house mentioned in verse 10, then perhaps the children of the host were being brought to Jesus, possibly at bedtime. Mark says that those who brought them desired Jesus to "touch" them. Matthew explains that this involved laying his hands on them and praying (Matt. 19:13). The Twelve, however, were irritated by this interruption. Doubtless they wanted to spare Christ from what they regarded as an annoyance. They also selfishly resented having Jesus distracted from His discussions with them. They felt His time was too valuable to be wasted on children.

Jesus, however, was displeased with the disciples' disregard of children. The Greek verb used by Mark to

---

[1]France, R. T. *The Gospel of Mark,* in *The New International Greek Commentary* series (Grand Rapids: Eerdmans, 2002), 388.
[2]Ibid.

describe Christ's response actually means "to be indignant." He ordered the disciples to stop hindering the children, and made it clear that His ministry included children in its scope. He went even further by showing that all who would be true followers of Him must possess certain childlike qualities. How different this is from our usual thinking! We so often reverse this and suppose that children must become like adults in order to enter the kingdom of God. Jesus, however, emphasized the need for all persons to possess childlike trust and loving submission and obedience in order to be born into the kingdom.

## Teaching about Wealth, 10:17–31

### The Rich Man, 10:17–22

As Jesus resumed His journey toward Jerusalem, presumably still in Perea, He was confronted by a man who ran to Him and knelt before Him. Matthew 19:20, 22 says the man was young (Mark notes that he was running), and Luke 18:18 says he was a ruler, presumably a synagogue ruler. He asked Jesus what he could do to inherit eternal life. He was evidently convinced that he did not then possess it and that it could be obtained only by performing something good.

Before Jesus could help him, the man needed to have the proper estimation of Jesus. Jesus asked him, therefore, "Why do you call me good?" If the man saw Jesus as merely a good man in a relative sense, there was nothing Jesus could do for him that other counselors could not. Our Lord certainly was not denying His own goodness or deity, but He wanted the man to see that it wasn't enough to recognize Him merely as "good." Because of some of the claims Jesus made, it should be obvious that if He were not God, then He was not even good, for some of His claims would be false.

Our Lord then picked out commandments from the second portion of the Ten Commandments (which He later summarized as the "second" commandment, Matt. 22:36–40), for violations of these are the most obvious. Inasmuch as the man was interested in deeds, Jesus called his attention to these God-given regulations as a starting point for the discussion. Jesus did not mean that life was to be gained by law-keeping but that a careful look at the Law should reveal a man's failure. When the man said he had kept all the regulations of the Law since his youth, he revealed that he had the common, superficial view of sin, supposing that sin consisted only of external acts. Because he had not violated these regulations in actual deed, he imagined he was in the clear.

Christ saw great potential in this misguided but attractive young man. He therefore pointed out the key to his problem with the hope that the man would respond to the challenge. He knew that the great love of the man's life was his possessions, and He asked him to sell them, dispense the proceeds to the poor, and become a follower of Jesus. (Jesus did not make this same demand of all others. He was merely calling attention to the thing that was keeping this man from full commitment.) Unfortunately, the man was not willing to do what Jesus asked. But he did learn that eternal life demands a total commitment to Christ, a commitment he was not now willing to make. This is the only instance in the Gospels when Jesus' direct invitation to follow Him was rejected.

## The Disciples, 10:23–27

When the rich man left, Jesus used the incident for further comment to His disciples. He emphasized the great difficulty the wealthy have in entering the kingdom of God. These words astonished His followers, for they ran counter to usual Jewish thinking. It was commonly supposed that riches were a mark of divine favor and that the rich had natural advantages in the spiritual realm just as they did in most other realms. Yet Jesus indicated that riches may well be a handicap rather than an advantage.

The proverb, "It is easier for a camel to go through an eye of a needle," contrasts the largest beast in Palestine with the smallest of apertures. (Efforts to explain "camel" as a misspelling of the Greek word for "rope" have no valid textual support, and to explain "needle's eye" as a gate for pedestrians into the city of Jerusalem has no archaeological basis.) The point of the proverb is not that it is hard, but that it is impossible to accomplish this feat apart from supernatural intervention (see v. 27).

This line of truth was astonishing to the disciples. They must have thought: If even rich men with all their advantages find it impossible, how can anyone at all be saved? Jesus then made the point that was vital for the whole discussion. Salvation is not a matter of doing good things or possessing natural advantages. Only God is able to bring salvation to men, whether they be rich or poor. Every man needs to stop trusting his wealth, or his efforts, and turn in faith to the forgiving grace of God, who has provided salvation in Christ.

**Peter, 10:28–31**

Peter now began to compare himself (and the rest of the Twelve) favorably with the rich man, for he and the others had done what Jesus had required of him. Surely, he thought, he and the others should be able to expect great reward. Jesus acknowledged that real sacrifices had been made and they would not go unnoticed. He mentioned a series of things that are deeply involved in a man's life and that he may have to forsake in order to follow Christ. (The term "wife" was wrongly included in the KJV in verse 29, but it is not found in the best Greek texts.)

Christ then promised to make up in vastly more generous ways whatever has been sacrificed for Him. Although some of this compensation is to be enjoyed in this life, we are reminded that persecutions will also be part of the present experience (only Mark mentions the persecutions). But in the life to come, the eternal life we possess will reach its consummation as even our bodies will receive their glorification. Much of Christ's compensation is spiritual,[3] however, and thus not always recognized by all men. Consequently, human evaluations may suffer reversal when Christ's rewards are fully given. Some Christians who presently seem to be unrewarded will have the greatest rewards.

## Third Prediction of Jesus' Death and Resurrection, 10:32–34

The phrase, "On the road, going up to Jerusalem" (v. 2), may imply the actual uphill journey from the Jordan Valley

---

[3]The mention of "one hundred times as much" was hardly meant to be regarded as literal (one hundred times as many mothers, children, brothers, and sisters?).

to Jerusalem, a climb of more than 3,000 feet in less than twenty miles. However, a trip to Jerusalem is regularly described as "going up," regardless of compass direction,[4] and that seems to be Mark's intention here. The actual climb into the Judean ridge would not begin until after they had left Jericho, and this had not yet occurred (see v. 46). Thus they seem to be somewhere between Perea and Jericho but headed for Jerusalem.

As Jesus and the disciples continued their trip toward Jerusalem, Jesus apparently walked in front of the group. There is also mention of an additional group, "those who followed" (v. 32), although some have explained these as including the Twelve. The fact, however, that Jesus "took the Twelve aside" implies that He was separating them from others for the purpose of giving them some special information. The remaining followers were fearful. They knew of the current unrest and hostility toward Jesus in the city and were apprehensive of what might happen.

Jesus then took the Twelve aside, and for the third time, He gave a clear prediction of His approaching death (see 8:31, 9:31).[5] Both previous announcements had met with resistance, rejection, or at least incomprehension, and thus there was the need for repeated instruction. A number of additional details were given at this time. Jesus implied that His death would occur during this visit to Jerusalem. He also mentioned that the Gentiles would have a part in His death. By stating that the Gentiles would mock, spit, scourge, and kill, He was virtually saying the Romans would crucify Him; for Romans were the only Gentile officials in Jerusalem, and

[4]See John 2:13, 5:1, and 11:55 as examples of this practice.
[5]The previous predictions are in 8:31 and 9:31.

crucifixion was their method of execution. Matthew's parallel account actually uses the word "crucify" (Matt. 20:19).

## Request of James and John, 10:35–45

James and John were among the very first disciples chosen by Jesus. Matthew indicates that their request was actually voiced by their mother (Matt. 20:20). Her name was Salome, and she may have been a sister of Jesus' mother (compare Matt. 27:56 with Mark 15:40 and John 19:25). If so, these brothers were first cousins of Jesus.

Their blank check request surely indicated their trust in Christ's sovereignty, but the content of the request showed a woeful lack of appreciation for the announcement Jesus had just made. They were desirous of the positions of highest honor in His coming messianic kingdom, and the request seems bold and ill-timed. Yet, it does show their genuine faith that somehow Christ's kingdom was real and imminent. Perhaps this is why Jesus did not deal with them harshly.

Jesus indicated that their request was based on a superficial regard for the factors involved. Before the honor there must come the cross. The "cup" was an Old Testament symbol of suffering (Isa. 51:17). "Baptism" (Greek: *baptisma*) is used by Jesus as another idiom for extreme suffering. Thus, Jesus revealed that His followers would experience something like the suffering He must undergo (although, of course, without any atoning implications). Suffering was fulfilled in the later lives of James and John, as James was the first of the Twelve to be martyred (Acts 12:1–2) and John suffered various imprisonments and an exile (Rev. 1:9). Jesus then explained that such favors were not to be awarded capriciously. The Father in heaven had the prerogative of bestowing these honors, and He would do it on the basis of faithful service, not because of favoritism.

The other ten disciples were indignant that two of their group had sought personal advancement beyond the rest. To them Jesus explained that worldly governments are organized on the principle of rank, with the exercise of authority proceeding from the top. He did not dispute the appropriateness of this principle in civil government, but He did explain that His kingdom had a different principle. It is not wrong for a believer to desire excellence and leadership in the Lord's work ("whosoever wishes to become great among you," v. 43). But the method of achieving greatness in Christ's cause is faithful service.

The greatest example of this principle was Jesus Himself, who "did not come to be served, but to serve" (v. 45). His greatest service was about to be performed in Jerusalem when He would give His life as "a ransom for many." This statement is not a contrast between "many" and "all," as though He were saying He was just going to die for some, but not all. Rather it is a contrast between the "one" who would die and the "many" who would be saved. Of course, the death of Christ was the atoning sacrifice for the whole world (1 John 2:2), even though the benefits of salvation are received only by those who believe (John 3:16).

## The Healing of Bartimaeus, 10:46–52

This miracle occurred at Jericho, a city about fifteen miles from Jerusalem. Mark and Matthew say Jesus met Bartimaeus as He went out from Jericho, but Luke says it was as He entered. The accounts may be harmonized by understanding two Jerichos—the ruins of the Old Testament city, and the presently occupied site about two miles south where Herod had built a winter palace—with the miracle occurring as Jesus left the site of the former and was approaching the latter.

Fig. 11. New Testament Jericho in foreground (excavation of Herod's winter palace). Two miles north is the site of Old Testament Jericho (see mound in upper left center).

Bartimaeus was apparently the spokesman for himself and a blind companion (Matt. 20:30). Having learned that Jesus was passing by, he cried out for help. By calling Jesus "son of David," he was using a recognized messianic title, and Jesus accepted it. Earlier in His ministry Jesus had not desired such titles to be used because of the likelihood of political overtones. Now, however, the time was growing short, and the strong hostility from official sources made any widespread political movement based on mere popularity most unlikely.

Attempts of the crowd to quiet his outcries were unsuccessful. Perhaps they were in a hurry to push on to the city to obtain lodging. Jesus, however, stopped in His tracks and summoned Bartimaeus, who jumped up at once and came to Him. Our Lord then asked that he state what he wanted. This not only caused the man to define his need, but also caused the crowd to realize that he was not requesting alms but healing. As Bartimaeus explained that he desired his sight, he addressed Jesus as "Rabboni." This was a term of high respect, a stronger form of "rabbi." We remember it as the term used by Mary Magdalene when she saw Jesus at the garden tomb following His resurrection (John 20:16). It suggests that Bartimaeus's faith went deeper than this casual meeting along the road might otherwise suggest. Jesus Himself said the man's faith had saved him. Bartimaeus was immediately healed and joined the caravan to Jerusalem. He also became a follower of Jesus, experiencing both physical and spiritual salvation.

## Truths to Remember

• God Himself established marriage, and Jesus gave it His full endorsement.

• Christ may not require every believer to get rid of his possessions, but He does expect each to be willing to do so.

• Although Christians may expect troubles in this life, they will also receive blessings that more than compensate (10:30).

# Part III

## The Ministry in Jerusalem
### Mark 11:1–14:72

# 11

# THREE EVENTFUL VISITS TO THE CITY AND THE TEMPLE
## Mark 11:1–33

The largest single portion of each of the Gospels is devoted to the final week of Christ's life. The last six chapters of Mark describe this period. We commonly speak of it as Holy Week, or Crucifixion Week, or Passion Week (from the Greek word for "suffering"). These events bring us to the blackest hour in human history, when men reject the Son of God and send Him to the cross. The significance the Gospel writers attributed to these momentous days is indicated by the amount of space they devoted to describing them.

Yet the Gospels never let us forget that Jesus did not end His life as an unfortunate, whining victim. Each writer in his own way depicts our Lord as energetic, carefully planning His movements, and fully in control of every situation.

Not only were these final days of special theological significance, but they were also some of the most dramatic moments in Christ's ministry. Certain events of this week have captured the imagination of artists throughout the centuries. His cleansing of the temple was a majestic and forceful display of righteous wrath. The cursing of the fig tree with its startling physical consequences was a striking display of supernatural power. The confrontation with various groups in the temple set forth our Lord's matchless skill in rendering His opponents speechless, and in explaining the deepest truths with utmost clarity.

# The First Visit, 11:1–14

## The Triumphal Entry, 11:1–11

*The Instructions, 11:1–3.* Before starting out for Jerusalem, Jesus made some minute travel plans. This was in contrast to his usual practice, for there is no indication that Jesus ever rode during His travels except on this one occasion. He and the disciples had been at Bethany (see John 12:1). Now He sent two of His disciples (who are not identified further in any of the Gospels) to the nearby village of Bethphage (see Matt. 21:1). Apparently, Bethany and Bethphage were both on the far side of the Mount of Olives, not more than two miles from Jerusalem. This occasion provides the only New Testament mention of Bethphage, and its precise location is not known.

Christ instructed the two men to enter the village and find a certain colt tied. Matthew's account tells us the colt would be with its mother and they were to bring both animals. This would help to calm the unbroken colt. It was not uncommon for young animals to be employed for sacred purposes (Num. 19:2, Deut. 21:3, 1 Sam. 6:7). The disciples would naturally wonder whether they might be stopped in their attempt to take the animal, so Jesus anticipated the problem by giving them the answer to use. They were to tell the owner that "the Lord has need of it." Perhaps the owner was a believer who had given Jesus a blank-check offer of the animal whenever He might need it. "And immediately he will send it back here." This seems to have been Jesus' promise to return the animal to the owner as soon as His use of it was over.

*The Preparations, 11:4–7.* The two disciples followed Jesus' instructions and made preparations for the trip. They found everything precisely as Jesus had said. The colt was tied outside the doorway of a house along a street in the village. Just as Jesus explained, the two were questioned by some bystanders. Luke 19:33 specifies that these questioners were the owners, as their giving of permission also indicates (Mark 11:6). When the explanation was made, there was no further problem.

When they brought the colt to Jesus, they also placed their outer robes on it. This unridden colt would have had no other saddle. Perhaps these colorful trappings gave a semblance of royalty, or at least pageantry, to the whole proceedings. Jesus then mounted the colt and began His brief trip to Jerusalem. Why did Jesus do this? He usually walked, not rode. The distance was not far; He frequently walked much farther. Yet, on this occasion, He made elaborate preparation to ride. John's Gospel (12:14–16) makes it clear that Jesus was fulfilling Zechariah 9:9. So does Matthew's (21:4–5). This Old Testament prophecy foretold that Israel's Messiah would come, but it also indicated that His coming would be meek and lowly. Inasmuch as Jesus was going to be rejected and crucified, it was most appropriate that this particular prophecy be fulfilled at this time.

*The Procession, 11:8–10.* As Jesus and His companions headed for Jerusalem, they were accompanied by a larger group of friends and well-wishers. Many of them threw their outer robes onto the roadway and then spread them out as an act of homage to Jesus as He passed. It was the sort of gesture appropriate for royalty. Others brought leafy branches that they had cut from the fields nearby and used them to line the path as Jesus passed.

The crowds soon became so large that there were throngs in front of Jesus and others following along behind. John's Gospel explains that there were really two distinct groups—

one that accompanied Jesus from Bethany and another that had come out from Jerusalem to meet Him (John 12:12–18). The cries of "Hosanna" (literally "save, I pray") were based on Psalm 118:25–26. The words expressed high spiritual elation, and in this instance they were suggestive of Christ's unique saving mission. That the shouters were using the words in a messianic sense seems certain from the response of the Pharisees (Luke 19:39–40).

Just how much did these people understand what they were saying? Did they really think Jesus was about to set up the Davidic kingdom after more than 600 years? Where were these people a few days later when men were clamoring for His death and no one came forward in His defense? Even though it is quite likely that some of them were caught up in the enthusiasm of the hour, some at least could have held the true messianic hope and have longed for Jesus to establish that kingdom. There had been many prophecies that said the Messiah would be the king (for example, Micah 5:2). The wise men at the birth of Christ expressed the same hope (Matt. 2:2). The angel of the Annunciation had made this very clear to Mary (Luke 1:32–33). But even if the expectations of some were truly kindled, they must have died later when the enemies of Jesus moved swiftly toward His arrest, trial, and execution.

*The Arrival, 11:11.* It was late afternoon by the time Jesus entered the city. He proceeded directly to the temple, but He did nothing except to look around. The formal priestly functions were now over for the day. Undoubtedly He noticed the booths and stalls of the merchants, but He took no action on this first visit during Crucifixion Week.

Jesus then retired to Bethany with the Twelve. He may have gone to the home of friends there (Lazarus'?), or perhaps He spent the night outdoors on the Mount of Olives, which was beside Bethany. Luke 21:37 suggests that the latter was His practice during the nights of this week. Because Bethany was at the foot of the Mount of Olives, the two names were used somewhat interchangeably in the New Testament (cf. Luke 24:50 with Acts 1:12).

### Cursing the Fig Tree, 11:12–14

On the morning following the Triumphal Entry, Jesus and the disciples started out once again toward Jerusalem when He became hungry. If He had stayed with Lazarus, one would attribute His hunger to fasting, since food would have been available at the house. However, it seems clear that Jesus was planning to eat, and thus one wonders why Mary and Martha did not feed Him. It is probably better to understand that He had lodged outdoors on the slopes of Olivet (with Bethany at the foot), as Luke 21:37 indicates. Therefore, there was no ready means of obtaining breakfast.

In the distance Jesus noticed a fig tree in full foliage. One of the unusual things about a fig tree is that it produces an early crop of fruit at the same time its leaves appear. Even though it was early April, the presence of its full complement of leaves would lead one to expect fruit as well. However, when Jesus came to the tree, He found no fruit at all, only leaves. It seems clear that He expected to find figs and was disappointed when He did not. Even though it was too early for the usual fig crop ("it was not the season for figs"), the presence of the leaves indicated that this tree was further advanced than others.

This is an instance in which the omniscience of Jesus was not employed. When the divine Son of God became man, He "emptied Himself" (Phil. 2:7), in that He voluntarily placed Himself in a servant's position and was led by the Spirit during His earthly life. He used His powers of deity only when it was the clear intention of the Father that He do so. Consequently, on certain occasions He used His almighty power to still storms and perform other miracles, but on other occasions He became physically tired like other men (John 4:6). It is no denial of Christ's deity to see in His expectations regarding the fully leafed fig tree a perfectly normal human reaction, even though His expectation was not met. (This seems more likely than to suppose He was merely pretending to expect figs.)

Jesus pronounced a curse upon this tree that promised so much but provided nothing. It was to remain permanently fruitless. In view of the alarming information Jesus had given the disciples about His prospects in Jerusalem, this miracle of the fig tree may well have been intended to remind them that He was still the Son of God, and this should encourage them for the coming days. Many, however, see here an action that was somewhat parabolic.[1] Jesus had previously used the fig tree as a symbol of the Jewish nation (Luke 13:6–9). Her outward appearance of religion but utter absence of spiritual fruit would bring about her doom. (The outcome of this curse is described in verses 20–26.)

---

[1]Thomas and Gundry, *A Harmony of the Gospels*, 179 ftn.

# The Second Visit, 11:15–19

### Cleansing the Temple, 11:15–18

Jesus' second visit to Jerusalem occurred after the cursing of the fig tree but before its withering had been discovered. He and His party went into the city for the second straight day and went directly to the temple. On the previous day Jesus had merely looked around. Today it was a different story.

As one passed through the gates into the temple precincts, he first entered the Court of the Gentiles. This was a large, open-air courtyard in which anyone (Gentiles included) might enter. In it were stalls and booths used by merchants who sold animals for sacrifice. Money changers also had tables there for the purpose of exchanging Roman

Fig. 12. Model of the temple of Jesus' day. The court of the Gentiles is the open area inside the large outer walls in which Jesus drove out the merchants and money changers.

coinage for the special temple coins required for religious contributions. Although a case can be made for the necessity of providing such services for the worshipers, they did not need to be located in a place intended for worship.

Verse 16 contains a detail not found in any other Gospel. Apparently some were using the temple grounds as a shortcut across the city and thus had completely disregarded the sacred character of this area. Jesus dramatically stopped this traffic, overturned the bankers' tables, and drove out the merchants with their goods. Once before, at the beginning of His ministry, He had done the same thing (John 2:13–22), but the merchants and bankers had soon resumed business in the same old way. It is to the shame of the priests and the populace of Jerusalem that such an action needed to be repeated.

Jesus accompanied His remarkable action with scathing words of condemnation (v. 17) based on Isaiah 56:7. This Scripture passage had pronounced the temple to be a place of prayer. It was to be a worshipful place for all men, including the many Gentiles who came from time to time. Yet, it had become something far different. Jesus said, "You have made it a robbers' den" (cf. Jer. 7:11). He did not necessarily mean by this phrase that it was a place where robbery was committed (thieves do not rob in their own dens), but that it was a place where robbers hid. These men used the sanctity of the temple as a protection for evil deeds. Merely buying and selling in such a place was disturbing enough, but it is likely they were often dishonest as well. These bazaars were under the monopoly of the high priest, and the absence of competition usually brings exorbitant prices.

The officials of Judaism quickly heard what was going on. Their hostility increased, and they looked for ways to eliminate Jesus because they feared His growing popularity. Whenever the crowds listened carefully to His words, there was the possibility that they would become adherents of Jesus, and thus would look to Him instead of to them for spiritual and religious leadership. However, no action was taken against Him at this time.

### Withdrawal from the City, 11:19

When evening came, Jesus once again left the city and returned to the vicinity of Bethany. The use of "whenever" suggests this was His customary practice, not merely what happened on this one occasion. This is what He did each evening of that week (see v. 11).

## The Third Visit, 11:20–33

### The Withered Fig Tree Explained, 11:20–26

*The Results, 11:20–21.* After Jesus had cursed the fig tree the previous morning (see verses 12–14), He and the disciples went on to Jerusalem, where they spent the day. It was dark when they returned to Bethany (that is, the Mount of Olives), so they would not have noticed the condition of the fig tree. The next morning, however, as they once more headed for Jerusalem, they passed by the same tree in broad daylight. It was dead. Peter's exclamation, "Rabbi, behold the fig tree!" was not a reproach but an expression of amazement at the prompt response of the tree to Jesus' command. It had not merely remained fruitless; within twenty-four hours it had withered to its very roots (v. 21).

*The Need for Faith, 11:22–24.* Peter's exclamation seems to imply that the prompt response that came from heaven in answer to Jesus' command was something ordinary men could not experience. Jesus used the incident to teach about effective prayer.

He pointed out that one must have faith in God if he is to expect answers to his prayers. God honors faith, and without faith it is impossible to please Him (Heb. 11:6). One must believe in the power and will of God in regard to the thing prayed for. As Jesus spoke these words, the group was standing in the vicinity of the Mount of Olives. So, His reference to "this mountain" in His illustration probably referred to the mount nearby. The striking statement (which may have been a proverb) that the mountain could be cast in the sea by faith was meant to teach the disciples that God is able to remove difficulties in their ministries that could not be removed in any other way.

One should be careful to note precisely what Jesus said. He did not say that an optimistic spirit or a positive mental attitude is all that is required. What is needed is "faith," and faith is a great deal more than a purely subjective condition. In the Bible, faith refers to man's response to what God has revealed. One can ask in faith after he understands what God's will is. Unless one knows that it is God's will that the mountain be removed, he can hardly pray in faith that it be done. So Jesus said that praying in faith involves believing "that what he says is going to happen." But if God hasn't said it, then to make such a request and call it faith is not faith at all; it is presumption. It is the believer's blessed privilege, however, to place the utmost confidence in what God has shown His will to be, and to ask in unwavering faith that God remove the obstacles that stand in the way of performing God's will.

*The Need for a Forgiving Spirit, 11:25–26.* Another essential for effective praying is a right attitude. Every time we pray, we need to be conscious of who we are. We are sinners in the presence of a holy God. Even as believers we need to confess our sins, in order that our prayers may be unhindered (Ps. 66:18). Yet, an unforgiving spirit toward others is itself sinful and needs to be confessed. Jesus did not say we should wait until the offender has confessed to us or has repented. We should forgive at once and not harbor a spirit of bitterness or revenge. (Verse 26 is not found in our most ancient manuscripts, but the same thought is expressed in Matt. 6:15.)

### Questioning of Jesus in the Temple, 11:27–33

*The Question, 11:27–28.* For the third consecutive morning Jesus entered the city of Jerusalem and went to the temple. He soon had a group around Him listening to His words and asking Him questions. This doubtless took place in the open Court of the Gentiles, which was large enough for great throngs of people. The group that accosted Jesus was made up of three elements (chief priests, scribes, and elders), and these formed the Sanhedrin. This was the highest governing body of the Jews and was allowed by Rome to exercise control over most internal affairs. The entire Sanhedrin consisted of seventy members in addition to the high priest, who acted as president. It was representatives of this body who confronted Jesus and questioned His authority. They may have consulted together since the events of the temple cleansing the day before. They wanted to know what right He had to do such things.

*The Counter Question, 11:29–30.* A good teacher often answers a question by employing a counter question to stimulate the thinking of the inquirer. Thus, Jesus was not evading their question but calling attention to a relevant case. If they would answer His question honestly, it would provide them with the answer to their own.

Jesus asked them about the ministry of John the Baptist, referring to its most striking feature—the baptism he performed. Had it been divinely commissioned, or was it a mere human arrangement? Inasmuch as Jesus and John were in perfect harmony, the answer to this question would be the answer to the other.

*The Dilemma, 11:31–32.* Either of the two alternatives by which the questioners might answer would destroy them. If they admitted that John was a heaven-sent messenger, then Jesus could ask the embarrassing question, "Why didn't you believe John?" But since John had pointed the people to Jesus as the Lamb of God (John 1:29), to believe John would obligate one to believe Jesus. On the other hand, to deny that John was divinely commissioned would run counter to the general attitude of the Jews, and these politicians were most sensitive to such matters.

*The Result, 11:33.* Unable to escape the dilemma, by either choosing one of the alternatives or suggesting a third solution, they refused to make any answer at all. Therefore, Jesus refused to answer their question, also. This was not stubbornness on His part. Rather, when the Sanhedrin refused to commit itself on John, it was refusing to accept John's testimony regarding Jesus. Jesus was under no obligation to give more authorization for Himself, since they had refused the authorization God had already sent by way of John.

## Truths to Remember

• Although Jesus was consciously fulfilling Zechariah 9:9 and thus claiming to be Israel's king, He had no illusions that the nation was going to accept Him. The use of the donkey indicates His understanding of the lowliness of the king at this stage of His program.

• Effective prayer requires trust in God's revealed will.

• Even in the deepening shadows of Crucifixion Week, the sovereignty of Christ is evident for those with eyes to see.

# 12

## TEACHING IN THE TEMPLE
### Mark 12:1–44

Jesus continued His last day of teaching in the temple by responding to questions put to Him by various groups. The first of those groups was composed of chief priests, scribes, and elders (11:27), and after answering their question, Jesus gave a parable that illustrated most effectively the point He had been making

The stories Jesus used to illustrate His teaching or to convey new truth were drawn from the activities of everyday life. He was not the inventor of using parables as teaching devices, but it is commonly recognized that Jesus was the master of the parable. No one in all literature used parables so effectively as He. These simple stories were understandable by all and portrayed with great clarity some of Christ's most important truths.

When Jesus explained the meaning of Old Testament passages, He saw meaning there that had escaped all other rabbis. He found messianic implications in many references that none had seen before.

### Parable of the Wicked Vine-Growers, 12:1–12

The Parable of the Wicked Vine-Growers further answers the question of Jesus' authority (11:27–28) by showing Him as the divine Son sent by the Father. Mark says He "began to speak to them in parables," but lists only this one. Matthew records two others (Two Sons, Matt. 21:28–32; and Marriage of the King's Son, Matt. 22:1–14).

The main lines of this parable are so clear that the Sanhedrin members who were questioning Jesus could hardly have failed to get the point. The story is about a man who planted a vineyard. This undoubtedly reminded the hearers of Isaiah 5:1–7, which depicted the nation of Israel as God's vineyard. Another Old Testament passage that uses the same imagery is Psalm 80:8–16.

Fig. 13. A vineyard watchtower in Samaria.

The owner placed a fence around the vineyard. In the parable this depicted God's separating Israel from the nations of the world for her own spiritual well-being. The winepress consisted of two vats—a higher one for treading the grapes, and a lower one into which the extracted juice ran by way of a spout. This well-planned vineyard also had a watchtower for the protection of the crop. When the owner had made every conceivable provision for the safety and prosperity of the vineyard, he leased it to some vine growers while he was absent. This depicted the Jewish rulers who were entrusted with the care of God's people prior to Christ's coming.

According to the story, the agreement between the owner and the vine-growers was that the owner should receive a certain portion of the crop. Therefore, at the season of harvest (or else at the season previously agreed upon for settlement), the owner sent a servant to obtain his due. The servant was beaten and sent away with nothing. The same treatment, but with increased severity, was meted out to the next emissary. These two were followed by a succession of messengers, but they were no more successful than the first, and some of them lost their lives in the process. As outrageous as this lawless action was, it was no worse than Israel's treatment of the prophets whom God sent to her through the centuries. (See these Old Testament passages for examples of Israel's action toward the prophets: Jer. 20:1–2, 37:15, 38:6; 1 Kings 19:10, 22:24; 2 Chron. 24:21.)

Finally, the owner decided to stop sending servants and send his beloved son. Here is a picture of God's incredible grace in view of what had previously happened to the prophets. The extraordinary patience of the owner reveals more clearly the depravity of the vine-growers. They foolishly reasoned that if they could do away with the rightful heir, they could then possess the property. This was precisely the attitude expressed by Caiaphas toward Jesus in John 11:47–53.

From this point on, the parable becomes prophetic. It foretells how shamefully the son would be killed. Jesus then asked a question (v. 9) that forced the hearers to come to the obvious conclusion in view of the facts presented. Matthew indicates that the audience actually spoke the answer (Matt. 21:41). The destruction of the vine-growers and their replacement by others depicted the coming judgment upon Israel that occurred in A.D. 70. This resulted in the complete elimination of the current Jewish leadership. These utterly worthless religious heads were removed, and a new spiritual body was formed. The true spiritual remnant within Israel were brought to faith in Christ and became part of a new body, Christ's Church.

In verses 10 and 11 Jesus reminded His listeners of the passage in Psalm 118:22–23, the very Psalm from which the "hosannas" shouted by the crowds were derived. It was a Psalm regarded as messianic by the Jews, and Jesus here applied it to Himself. He was the Son, sent by the owner of the vineyard and rejected by the vine-growers. But He would become the most significant stone of a new building, in spite of being rejected by His nation.

The result was that the truth struck home to these religious leaders. However, it did not produce repentance, but further antagonism.

## Questioning by Pharisees and Herodians, 12:13–17

It appears that "they" in verse 13 are the Sanhedrin of verse 12. They planned their strategy so that individual groups might discredit Jesus in the eyes of the people (see Luke 20:20). They hoped to prod Him into speaking ill-advisedly, trapping Himself with argument.

The Pharisees and the Herodians had little in common except their antagonism toward Jesus. Pharisees were traditionalists in religion, holding to the very letter of the Mosaic Law as well as the traditions handed down by the rabbis. On this matter of paying tribute to Rome, which they were questioning, they would have opposed in principle any submission to foreign domination. The Herodians, however, were a group who supported the family of the Herods, who were non-Jewish and thus would have no deep-seated opposition to taxation. Both groups united in their hope that Jesus would discredit Himself by His answer to the question they posed.

The flattering introduction with which they approached Jesus would have been admirable if meant sincerely, for it was all true. Jesus did speak God's truth without partiality or favoritism. Such compliments inflate the egos of human teachers, cause them to glow with pride, and thus sway their judgment. This may have been the purpose of the speakers.

Their question, "Is it lawful to pay a poll-tax to Caesar?" meant, "In view of our obligation to God, is it spiritually right to acknowledge submission to a pagan government by paying taxes?" They hoped to cause Jesus either to speak treasonably against Rome, or else to take a view unpopular with the people.

Jesus dealt with the dilemma with a dramatic action. Calling for a Roman coin ("a denarius"), He asked whose image was marked on this Roman coinage, so that the answer could not be evaded. Yet by answering Jesus' question, His antagonists themselves provided the principle involved in the problem. Roman coinage was issued to facilitate commerce in the empire, and taxes paid for services supplied by Rome. Hence, every believer is obligated for his share in civil taxes (see Rom. 13:1–7). He is also obligated to perform his spiritual duties, but payment of taxes is no violation of these.

## Questioning by Sadducees, 12:18–27

The next group to heckle Jesus was the Sadducees. This party in Judaism was smaller than the Pharisees, but it was entrenched in the priesthood and was rich and powerful. Theologically speaking, the Sadducees were rationalists who denied spirit beings and physical resurrection (Acts 23:8). Their question was not really a request for information but an attempt to show the absurdity of traditional Jewish opinion about resurrection, which they were sure Jesus also held.

Their question was based on the Jewish law of levirate (or "brother-in-law") marriage as recorded in Deuteronomy 25:5–6. This law specified that in such cases the first child of the new marriage would be counted as the dead brother's. It was to insure that the family inheritance would not be broken up.

The Sadducees told of seven brothers, the first of whom married but died without children. Each surviving brother performed the levirate custom but died without producing children. Finally the wife died, also. This seems like a contrived story, but Jesus did not argue this point with them. When they finished relating this rather incredible series of events, they then came to the point. They were not questioning the Mosaic principle of levirate marriage. It was the resurrection aspects that they opposed.

The point of their whole story was this: Whose wife would the woman be if there really is such a thing as resurrection? Each brother had been married to her, and there were no children from any of the unions to prejudice the decision. Of course, the Sadducees did not believe in any physical resurrection at all, and they supposed that their little story illustrated the hopeless absurdity of such a doctrine.

Jesus replied that their problem was their failure to understand the Scripture and their underestimation of God's power. They did not grasp the clear Old Testament teaching on physical resurrection. Furthermore, they limited the power of God as being able to reproduce only the present order of existence. They failed to realize that God can resurrect physically and still make innovations.

Jesus went on to explain that with resurrected bodies men do not marry, nor are women given in marriage to men. They will be like angels, in that they will not exercise such functions as reproduction and childbirth. Apparently the number of angels was fixed at creation, so there has been no need for additional ones. Likewise, in the resurrection there will be no need for humans to be born, since none of the resurrected saints will ever die. Note that Jesus did not assert that believers will become angels in the life to come. He said that the relationship between men and women in the resurrection will not be the same as the marriage relation on earth, but will be as the relation between angels. The problem of the Sadducees was that they limited God's power to a mere reestablishment of earthly conditions.

Our Lord then pointed His listeners to the passage in Exodus 3:6, which they knew well. Inasmuch as God identified Himself to Moses as the God of Abraham, Isaac, and Jacob—men who had been physically dead for hundreds of years—it is clear that they continued to have existence after death. However, this was not precisely the point that was being argued. The point was, Do men rise physically after death? When Jesus said, "He is not God of dead ones but of living ones" (literal translation), He meant that physical death was not the final issue. If physical death cannot be superseded, then God has been thwarted in His plan to overcome the penalty of sin. But God is not the God of dead ones, but of living ones. When He claimed to be the God of Abraham, He meant the person of Abraham, which included all constituent parts, not just the soul. Full existence of the person ultimately requires the presence of all its basic elements. Even though God had spoken those words about Abraham before the resurrection, Jesus took them to imply that Abraham's physical resurrection would take place in due season.

Sometimes Christians are troubled by this teaching of Jesus, especially when a beloved husband or wife has gone to be with the Lord. They regard the absence of marriage in heaven as an unwelcome prospect. We must beware of making the same mistake as the Sadducees in limiting the power of God, as though all He can do is restore the present relationships. We need to accept by faith what Scripture reveals—that the new relationship in heaven will be even more wonderful than the most precious of relationships on earth.

## Questioning by a Scribe, 12:28–34

Scribes were experts in the Law of Moses and in the rabbinical regulations which had been handed down through the generations. Matthew indicates that the scribe who now questioned Jesus was a Pharisee and a lawyer (Matt. 22: 34–35). He would have been pleased with Jesus' answer to the Sadducees, for the Pharisees believed what Jesus taught about resurrection.

The scribe asked Jesus what was the most important commandment. There does not seem to be any unfriendly purpose involved in his question. In addition to the Ten

Commandments, Jewish rabbis counted 613 commands, which they regarded as a hedge about the Law. The relative importance of these was frequently disputed. The scribe wanted Jesus' opinion.

Jesus first cited Deuteronomy 6:4–5, which acknowledged who God is and commanded the devotion of men out of their whole being. This passage was a summarization of the first table of the Mosaic Law. The first portion (Deut. 6:4) was recited daily by pious Jews and is known as the "Shema" (from the opening Hebrew word).

Jesus then quoted Leviticus 19:18, which commanded love of one's neighbor. This summarizes the second table, containing man's duties to his fellows. Modern liberalism emphasizes love of neighbor but usually fails to note that this must be based squarely on the love of God. Otherwise, it is mere sentimentality. Jesus combined both aspects as composing "the foremost commandment" that the scribe wanted to know.

The scribe was impressed with the rightness of Jesus' answer and restated the same truth himself. It had been clearly taught in the Old Testament prophets, and the scribe seems to have accepted it sincerely. However, it is one thing to recognize a truth, but it is something else to commit oneself to it and act in the light of it. Jesus saw in this man a keen intelligence and real spiritual perception, and He commented, "You are not far from the kingdom of God." Inasmuch as the scribe recognized what God requires, he should have taken the next step.

These encounters left Jesus in complete command of the situation. No one had been able to ruffle His composure or confuse Him in argument. No one else stepped forward to try.

## Christ's Question about David's Words, 12:35–37

Into the silence that followed, Jesus injected His own question. He referred to the interpretation taught by all orthodox scribes that the Messiah would be David's son (that is, a descendent of David). He pointed to the Davidic Psalm containing these words: "The Lord said to my Lord, Sit at my right hand, until I put thine enemies beneath thy feet" (Ps. 110:1). In this Psalm Jehovah is depicted as saying to Messiah (this was the regular Jewish interpretation) that He should have a divine position. Yet in this Psalm David called Messiah "my Lord" (*Adonai*), in spite of the fact that He would be David's physical descendant and thus dependent upon David, not superior to him, in Jewish thinking.

The answer to the problem was that David must have regarded this messianic descendant of his as something more than just an ordinary man. He called Him "my Lord" because he recognized Him to be deity, entitled to sit at the right hand of Jehovah. Thus, Scripture itself presents the truth of the deity of Messiah, and it was David himself, who was the physical ancestor of Jesus, who said so. Matthew tells us that the scribes were silenced by this penetrating interpretation of Scripture (Matt. 22:46). The multitude of ordinary people thoroughly "enjoyed" Christ's teaching, however, and was not at all upset at seeing the "experts" silenced.

## Denunciation of the Hypocritical Rich and Commendation of a Poor Widow, 12:38–44

In His continuing teaching, our Lord directly warned against the hypocrisy that can so easily take hold of men and that was particularly exemplified by the rich and powerful, who often made a great pretense of piety. Even some of the religious scribes were guilty of this. These men loved ostentatious display and deference that their opulent dress elicited from the people. Elaborate and effusive greetings, which they exchanged in public places, called attention to their importance. They zealously sought to occupy places of honor in synagogues and at banquets. At the latter, to be seated near the host was a mark of special distinction.

Yet, these same people did not hesitate to "devour widows' houses." This refers to the evil practice of bilking widows out of their estates, perhaps by surreptitious counseling. At this time Jesus was in the part of the temple known commonly as the Court of the Women, or the Treasury. Into this area any Jew might come, but Gentiles were excluded. The two names for this area were drawn from the fact that this was as far into the temple proper as women could go, and also that in this court were thirteen trumpet-shaped receptacles for receiving monetary contributions.[1] On this occasion Jesus was noting how a steady stream of worshipers was passing by the chests making their donations. Included were many rich people, whose offerings were of some size.

In striking contrast to the hypocrisy described above, our Lord's attention was drawn to one poor widow as she made her contribution. He was never so engrossed with the crowds that He failed to be aware of individuals. This woman cast in two coins, the smallest ones in use at that time (total value about one-fourth of a cent[2]). Jesus told His disciples that she

---

[1]These thirteen chests for charitable contributions were marked separately to indicate the purpose of the offerings. This fact could have enabled Jesus to note that the widow's contribution was not a lavish one. Edersheim, Alfred. *The Temple* (Grand Rapids: Eerdmans, reprinted 1950), 48–49.

[2] Arndt and Gingrich notes that the Greek term *kodrantēs* used here for "cent" was a loanword from the Latin *quadrans*, and that its value was approximately one quarter of a cent in normal times. *A Greek-English Lexicon*, (Chicago: University of Chicago Press, 2nd ed., 1958), 4378.

had put in more than all the others. He did not deny that the rich had given much, but He stated that this widow had done even more. The reason was that the rich had given out of their surplus, so theirs was no real sacrifice. Jesus had apparently drawn upon His supernatural knowledge to ascertain that the woman's gift constituted the totality of her possessions. Thus, it was the quality of the gift, not its quantity, that made it "more" (v. 43).

## Truths to Remember

• Jesus foretold even to His enemies precisely what they were going to do to Him.

• Man has duties both to God and to country, and except in rare cases of conflict, God expects us to fulfill both.

• A right relationship with God is essential for right relations with men.

# 13

## THE OLIVET DISCOURSE
### Mark 13:1–37

The Olivet Discourse probably deserves to be called the greatest prophetic sermon ever given. In it our Lord describes the momentous events connected with His coming in glory, along with an explanation of the fortunes of the disciples during the intervening days of His absence. The sermon is based upon some biblical information previously given in the Old Testament, but adds considerably more detail in certain areas.

Some of the most difficult of Jesus' utterances are contained in this message. In form it is similar to the apocalyptic prophecies in the Old Testament, where the mingling of historical, prophetic, literal, and symbolic elements makes interpretation of details very difficult. For this reason (along with others), there has been much disagreement about the meaning of this sermon. Some have explained the prophetic elements as completely fulfilled within the forty years that followed, ending with the destruction of Jerusalem in A.D. 70. Others regard the sermon as describing the Church Age and a tribulation through which the Church must pass before Christ returns.

However, Jesus' language is parallel in many places to the prophetic descriptions in Daniel and Revelation. It seems that the primary subject of the sermon is equivalent to what Daniel's prophecy calls the "seventieth week" (Dan. 9:24–27), as it describes the period between the return of

Christ for His church (the rapture) and His actual coming to earth to establish the millennial kingdom. One very small portion of the sermon does describe the present age.

The most complete record of the Olivet Discourse is found in Matthew 24 and 25. More condensed accounts are given in Luke 21 and here in Mark 13. Unfortunately, the shorter accounts are often neglected.

## The Setting, 13:1–4

It was the end of that busy day of teaching in the temple (the subject of the previous chapter) when Jesus prepared to leave its precincts and retire to the Mount of Olives as He apparently had done each evening that week. This was His final departure from the temple. He never reentered it before the Crucifixion or after it, as far as we know.

Fig. 14. View of Jerusalem and the Temple Mount from the Mount of Olives.

As Jesus and His disciples left, one of them (other Gospels indicate he was joined by his companions) commented on the architectural beauty of the temple. This edifice built by Herod was known far and wide for its beauty and excellent construction. It had been under construction for nearly fifty years by this time (John 2:20) and was still not finished.[1] It was a cause of much national pride among the Jews.

In response, Jesus called attention to the remarkably sturdy buildings, some of whose stones were more than thirty feet long, and stated that the whole edifice was going to be demolished. Here was a direct prophecy that was fulfilled in A.D. 70, when the Roman army under Titus destroyed the temple and the city. Today a Mohammedan shrine, the Dome of the Rock, occupies the site.

The disciples and Jesus had by now made their way across the Brook Kidron and had climbed the slopes of Olivet, which gave an impressive view of the temple. The disturbing announcement Jesus made about the destruction of the temple prompted four of the disciples to question Him about it. Before they had left the temple, Jesus spoke of the coming desolations of Jerusalem that would not be reversed until the arrival of messianic blessings (Matt. 23:37–39). The disciples wanted to know when these destructions would occur and also what would be the sign of His coming (Matt. 24:3). It was this request for information that drew from Jesus the Olivet Discourse.

---

[1] F. F. Bruce states, "The main part of the work was completed and consecrated in ten years, but other parts were still being carried out; in fact the finishing touches were not put to the whole enterprise until A.D. 63, only seven years before its destruction." *The Gospel of John* (Grand Rapids: Eerdmans, 1983), 76. See also Josephus, *Antiquities of the Jews*, xx. 9.7 and xvii.10.2.

Fig. 15. Columns of the Temple destroyed in A.D. 70, reused as steps in later construction.

# Future Events Prior to the "Abomination of Desolation," 13:5–13

### The First Half of the Tribulation, 3:5–8

Although the matters mentioned by Jesus in this portion of His address are somewhat general and have occurred from time to time ever since Jesus was here, a comparison with the fuller account in Matthew 24 and the order of the opening of the seals in Revelation 6 seems to link this section to the first half of the Tribulation.

Students of Daniel 9:24–27 understand that the final phase of the present age as revealed by God in prophecy consists of a period known as the "seventieth week," which has two clearly marked halves.[2] Premillennial interpreters generally understand this to be a period of seven years, divided into two periods of three and a half years each. In Revelation 6 the opening events of the first three and a half years are symbolically described as a series of seals being opened on a scroll. The significant thing to note is the striking similarity between the order of the items portrayed by the seals and the order of events in the Olivet Discourse. It is more clearly seen in the fuller account in Matthew but can be seen to a limited degree in Mark. In Revelation 6 the order is as follows: first seal, Antichrist; second seal, warfare; third seal, famine; fourth seal, death for one-fourth of the earth; fifth seal, martyrs.

In the Gospel of Matthew the first five items follow this same order (24:5–9). In the Gospel of Mark the account is more condensed, but the first two items are named in the same order as the seals (false messiahs, wars), and the next two (earthquakes, famines) correspond to seals four and three in reverse order (13:5–8). It is true that such things have been the experience of the world throughout much of its history, but the similarity to the seals seems more than coincidental, and therefore these events should be placed within the same time period as the seals of Revelation 6.

Jesus gave this information to answer the question regarding the characteristics of the end of the age and the coming of the messianic era. His answer was in perfect

---

[2]The viewpoint presented in this commentary is premillennial and dispensational. Although no principle used to interpret prophecy is without difficulties, the author finds the viewpoint stated above as offering the most straightforward understanding of the scriptural data. Postmillennialists, amillennialists, and some premillennialists will, of course, take a different view.

agreement with the prophecies of Daniel and the later ones of John (Book of Revelation). The establishment of the kingdom would be preceded by these cataclysmic events. Jesus called them "the beginning of birth pangs" (v. 8). They would be the opening events of the prophesied Tribulation, of which the worst phase would be the final three and a half years. Although the specific reference of these verses is to a period in the future, we do well to note an increase in such tendencies as the time draws nearer.

### The Present Age, 13:9–13

This corresponds to the portion given in Luke's account (21:12–24) but not found in Matthew. There it is stated to be "before all these things" that have to do with the distant future (Luke 21:12). It describes the present Church Age, which will be closed by the Rapture before the Tribulation (Daniel's seventieth week) begins.

Jesus first warned His disciples that they would personally undergo persecution. In their Jewish communities, they would be taken before councils and synagogues and would be beaten. This began to occur in Acts 4:3 and 5:18, 40. Later they would appear before governors and kings because of their faithful witness to Christ. The apostles experienced persecution under Herod (Acts 12:1–5), and later the apostle Paul appeared before Sergius Paulus, Gallio, Felix, Festus, Agrippa II, and high officials at Rome (Acts 13:7–12; 18:12–17; 24; 25; 26). Even though they were not usually pleasant experiences, as Jesus said, they did provide a most effective testimony of Christ and the gospel—more so than mere unhindered preaching would have done.

Verse 10 indicates that the gospel would need to be preached to all nations.[3] In Matthew 24:14 a similar statement is given in a context referring to the Great Tribulation. There it was called the "gospel of the kingdom," because during the Tribulation the proclamation will emphasize that the messianic kingdom is about to be established. In the Mark passage, however, the reference occurs in a section about the present age. The simpler term "gospel" is used because the proclamation of the gospel of salvation in Christ is the emphasis today, even though the task will not be completed until the end of the Tribulation, at which time the "kingdom" emphasis will be added.

Christ's followers were encouraged not to worry about what to say during those times of persecution when they would be taken before the authorities and would have no time to prepare (v. 11). Jesus promised them the direct inspiration of the Holy Spirit for such occasions.

One of the sobering aspects of persecution would be the betrayal of their own family members. Even the closest of friends will sometimes turn against one another in order to save their own lives. Believers are warned against the false notion that their faith will be generally respected. Just the opposite will be true. Persecution, which began soon after Christ's departure, has continued intermittently throughout Church history and will reach its most violent stage after the Rapture has removed the Church. It will then be directed against the saints who are won during the Tribulation, including the Jews who will then accept the Messiah. The

---

[3]This verse should not be used to teach that Christ cannot return for His church until the missionary enterprise has reached every person on earth. Even Paul could generalize on this theme, when he declared that even in his day the gospel "was proclaimed in all creation under heaven" (Col. 1:23).

mark of the truly saved man is his enduring faith and his refusal to apostatize (v. 13). This is not salvation based on endurance, but salvation demonstrated by endurance. If one is truly saved, he will endure, for God will enable him (Rom. 14:4; 1 John 2:19).

## Future Events Following the "Abomination of Desolation," 13:14–23

Jesus' mention of the "abomination of desolation" (v. 14) makes it certain that He was referring to the middle of Daniel's seventieth week (see Dan. 9:24–27). Thus, we are taken to the midpoint of the seven-year tribulation period, which begins the most terrible persecution of all. (Some versions omit the mention of Daniel in Mark 13:14, but there is no question that Daniel's prophecy is referred to by the "abomination" (cp. Matt. 24:15).

The event to which Jesus referred is some sort of religious desecration that the Antichrist will perform in the middle of the seven-year Tribulation. It would seem to be the outstanding sign that Jesus gave to the Twelve in answer to their request (v. 4). Premillenialists understand it to be the erection of an image of Antichrist in the restored Jewish temple (2 Thess. 2:4). Such blasphemy cannot be accepted by believers, and thus the greatest persecution of all will break out.

The Great Tribulation (the final three and a half years) will begin at Jerusalem, with the Abomination being the signal. At the time, residents of that area will need to flee from the spot to save their lives. The need for haste will be so pressing that there can be no delay for packing if a man wants to preserve his life. At this time, many Jewish homes had an outside stairway to a flat roof that was used for meditation and relaxation. Jesus warned that if a man receives the news while on the rooftop, he should flee at once. If he should happen to be working out in the fields clad only in his tunic, he should not take time to go back to his house to get his robe but should flee for his life immediately. Pregnant women and nursing mothers with small babies will have additional hardships when rapid flight is necessary. Inclement weather will also add to the difficulties.

What Jesus was describing was the greatest tribulation in the history of the world. This is why we know that He was speaking of the final Great Tribulation, not merely giving a general warning about hardships that have recurred from time to time. Daniel 12:1 speaks of the same thing. There have been great persecutions in the past, especially against the Jews, such as under Antiochus Epiphanes and, in modern times, under Adolf Hitler. Yet the one Jesus predicted here will be the worst of all. It was not fulfilled in the destruction of Jerusalem in A.D. 70, and has not happened yet. It will be promoted by Antichrist, and if God did not cut short the fulfillment of Antichrist's purpose, every believer would be killed. God is still sovereign, however; and in order to fulfill His purposes for His people, He will limit the days of tribulation.

When people are in such great distress, rumors abound. Even well-meaning people will clutch at straws if they seem to promise deliverance. Believers here are warned that any rumors that say Christ has already come and is to be found at some certain place are to be regarded as false. Nevertheless, false Christs and false prophets will arise. They will be satanically empowered, directed by the Antichrist, and able to produce supernatural wonders.

## The Return of Christ, 13:24–27

"In those days, after that tribulation" pinpoints the precise time of Christ's return as the end of the seven-year Tribulation. Consult Matthew 24:29–31 for another record of this prophecy.

The first event will be a series of changes in the heavens. The sun, moon, and stars will undergo great changes. There is no reason to understand these terms in any way other than literal. They describe a great upheaval and renovation of the universe in preparation for the Millennium. Such happenings were also foretold in Joel 3:15 and Isaiah 13:9–10.

The next event mentioned is the return of Christ in glory (v. 26). This is His actual return to the earth, accompanied by His Church, to establish His kingdom. Mark helps us to interpret a puzzling phrase in Matthew 24:30 where it is stated that there shall appear "the sign of the Son of man." Students have wondered whether this refers to some additional sign. However, since Mark in this parallel passage says merely that men shall see the Son of man coming in glory, it appears there will be no additional sign. In fact, the Son of man in glory is the sign. By seeing this momentous event, those on earth at that time will know that the Kingdom is about to begin.

The final event connected with the coming of Christ is the gathering of the elect from all parts of the earth (v. 27). These would seem to be the tribulation saints from the Gentile world who have been won to Christ since the Rapture and are alive at the time of Christ's return in glory. It would also include the gathering of the Jews. The Jewish aspect of this gathering seems to be twofold. There will be a national gathering of Jews, including unbelievers as well as believers (Ezek. 20:33–38). Then the unbelieving Jews will be removed, and the believing Jewish remnant will be left, along with the Gentile tribulation saints, to enter the Millennium.

## Warnings to Watchfulness, 13:28–37

### Parable of the Fig Tree, 13:28–31

The fig tree has the peculiar trait of producing fruit and leaves at about the same time. Thus, when the leaves are present, summer is near. The fig tree was also a frequent biblical symbol of the Jewish nation (Jer. 24, Joel 1:6–7, Hosea 9:10). It is disputed whether it is so used here. If so, then Jesus is saying that a revitalized Jewish nation is one of the indications that the Lord's coming is near. If this is not what it means here, then the sense is that just as leaves on a fig tree mean summer is near, so the beginning of the events previously described will mark the soon coming of Christ. All the events of the Tribulation will be completed within seven years.

The statement in verse 30, "This generation will not pass away until all these things take place," has been variously understood. The term "generation" can hardly mean Jesus' contemporaries, for, although they may have witnessed the destruction of Jerusalem, they certainly saw none of these end time events. The supernatural events in the heavens did not occur in their lifetime, nor did they witness the return of Christ in glory. Those who insist upon this interpretation must explain the striking changes in the heavens (vv. 24–25) as symbolic of political upheavals and view the return of Christ in a lesser way than literal.

Two other explanations are more reasonable. Jesus may have been referring to the generation that will be living at the end time, indicating that these events will occur so swiftly that the generation that sees the beginning of them will be the same generation to see their finish. Another possible explanation understands the Greek word here translated "generation" in its basic sense of "race" or "family." Thus, Jesus may have been saying that in spite of efforts to exterminate God's people from the earth (particularly the Jewish remnant), they will not be destroyed. God will still fulfill His promise to Abraham, and no effort of a Hitler (who killed six million Jews) or the final Antichrist will be completely successful. This "family" will be preserved as an entity to see the complete fulfillment of God's promises.

To reinforce the disciples' faith in the certainty of God's announced program, Jesus stated that His teaching was more permanent than the physical universe (v. 31). When He said that heaven and earth would pass away, He meant that this universe, which seems to us so indestructible, will eventually be superseded (Rev. 21:1, 2 Peter 3:10–11). These words of Christ, however, will never experience the slightest alteration. Such solemn assurances are the greatest source of comfort when we are tempted to think God's program is suffering defeat.

### Parable of the Door-Keeper, 13:32–37

The certainty of Christ's coming does not give us precise information as to the exact day and hour. Therefore, believers are always to be in a state of watchfulness and expectancy. Regardless of what phase of Christ's return applies to them — the rapture for the Church saint, or the return to earth in glory as awaited by Jewish and Gentile tribulation saints — all are to be ready.

Jesus said that the exact moment of His return in glory was known only by the Father in heaven. Neither angels nor Jesus Himself knew the time. Here was another instance in which Christ's self-limitation during His earthly career was evident. It may well be, however, that since His ascension and exaltation to the right hand of the Father, involving the resumption of the glory He had before the world was (John 17:5), He now possesses this knowledge.

The Parable of the Door-keeper is one of five that Jesus gave to conclude this discourse. Matthew records four of them, but only Mark includes this one. It describes a wealthy homeowner who left on a journey after giving to his servants various work assignments to accomplish during his absence. Among the servants was a door-keeper, whose task it was to guard the door, preventing unauthorized entrance and welcoming the owner when he returned. This story pictured Christ as ascended to heaven but having left His servants (believers) with responsibilities during His absence. Watchfulness obviously does not mean laziness, but rather faithful activity and alertness in anticipation of the Lord's return.

## Truths to Remember

• Only a God who can control the future can accurately foretell it. Otherwise, unforeseen changes might prove Him wrong. Yet the fulfillment of other divine prophecies testifies to God's power and wisdom.

• In spite of persecution of believers, God's program is not failing but moving according to His plan.

• There is no reason why the Rapture could not occur at any moment.

• Even in the deepening shadows of Crucifixion Week, the sovereignty of Christ is evident for those with eyes to see.

# 14

## THE FINAL HOURS
### Mark 14:1–72

Some of the most treasured hours of Christendom are recorded in this chapter. These were during the last evening before the Cross in which were packed some of Jesus' most significant words and deeds. It was during that evening that our Lord bared His heart before the disciples, giving some of the most profound teaching of His ministry. It was then that He instituted the symbols of foot-washing and the bread and cup while sharing a meal with the Twelve. The anguish in Gethsemane occurred on that last evening, where men are given a glimpse of the awesome spiritual battle that our redemption required.

The issues that had been raised by our Lord's remarkable ministry had come to a head. Although faith had been growing in the hearts of many, unbelief had also been developing and had become a hardened state among the religious authorities. This unbelief would produce the official rejection of Jesus as the Messiah of the Jews. We shall see just how widespread this sinful rejection was. We will note how Satan had so blinded the mind of Judas that he rejected Jesus for money. We shall also see how the Jewish authorities put Jesus on trial and how not one word was said in His defense. Those with the responsibility of guiding the nation in accord with the Mosaic Law utterly rejected the very one whom Moses had predicted would come (Deut. 18:15). On this final evening, the forces of spiritual darkness were so strong that rejection even manifested itself among the Twelve, as Peter denied his Lord three times and the whole group forsook Him and fled.

Yet the Gospels do not allow us to forget that He who was so shamefully rejected was still the majestic Lord whose dignity and composure never failed, and whose sovereignty shone through in remarkable ways during this unforgettable evening.

## The Plot, 14:1–11

The two feasts of Passover and Unleavened Bread would begin in two days. Passover occurred on the fifteenth of the month Nisan (with the lambs being slain on the afternoon of the fourteenth). It was followed immediately by the week-long festival of Unleavened Bread. Popularly, either name could be used for the entire festival.

The Jewish leaders recognized that feast time was crucial in their plans regarding Jesus. If there were to be any popular uprising to promote the messiahship of Jesus, then the forthcoming feast would probably be the time when it would be attempted. This must be headed off at all costs. Yet, the Sanhedrin leaders needed to proceed with caution because of Jesus' popularity with the common people, thousands of whom would be in Jerusalem for Passover. Their plot to do away with Jesus did not jell until Judas stepped forward with His offer.

Mark then recounts the details of the supper in Bethany. The chronology here is difficult because John puts this supper six days before Passover (John 12:1–2), but Mark and Matthew seem to place it only two days before. The best explanation is that Mark and Matthew are giving a flashback, because it was at this meal six days before Passover that the incident occurred that started Judas on his wicked scheme. Then, two days before Passover, after the Jews held their conference as to what to do about Jesus, Judas solved their problem by making his offer.

The supper in Bethany occurred at the house of Simon the leper (Matt. 26:6). Since it also seems to be the house of Mary, Martha, and Lazarus (John 12:2), numerous suggestions have been made to harmonize the references. Perhaps Simon was a relative, and Martha was called upon to do the hostess chores. If so, Simon must have been a healed leper, cured by Jesus during His ministry. Or perhaps he was like Uzziah, who had to live in separate quarters because of leprosy while his son ran the household (2 Chron. 26:21).

During the meal a woman (identified by John as Mary, the sister of Martha, John 12:3) broke an expensive vial of perfume and poured it upon Jesus' head and feet (John 12:3).[1] Some of the disciples were indignant at this apparent waste, but Judas was the instigator (John 12:4). The value of the perfume was in excess of 300 denarii (one denarius was a day's wage for a laborer, Matt. 20:2). To many in this group who had left much to follow Jesus, it seemed like a foolish, impulsive gesture.

Jesus, however, came to Mary's defense. He pointed out that what she did indicated an awareness of priorities and of

---

[1]There is no warrant for identifying this incident with the one in Luke 7:36–50. The event in Luke occurred much earlier in Galilee; the woman there is never named as Mary, and the fact that she was named as a sinful woman is contrary to every mention of Mary of Bethany. The fact that Simon is the name of the host in both contexts is mere coincidence. The name was extremely common in that day.

timing. There would continue to be abundant opportunities to do works of charity, but there were just a few days left to show love to Jesus directly. Mary had believed Jesus' predictions of His death on this trip to Jerusalem and realized that normal customs of respect would not be possible. As it turned out, this was the only burial anointing He received, for the women who came to do this after His death found that He had risen (16:1–6).

Two days later, Judas' disillusionment, which apparently became fixed at that meal four days earlier, now caused him to betray Jesus. He went to the priests with his offer to deliver Him at an opportune time.

## The Last Supper, 14:12–26

Jewish days begin at sundown, not at midnight, as ours do. The "first day of unleavened bread" refers to the day preceding the feast, when all leaven was removed from the houses and the Passover lambs were slain. Thus, twenty-four hours before the Passover meal was eaten, Jesus gave orders to two of the disciples (identified by Luke as Peter and John, Luke 22:8) to secure quarters for the group. They were to meet a man carrying a pitcher of water, follow him to a house, and then ask the owner, "The Teacher says, 'Where is My guest room…?'" (v. 14). It reads as if Jesus had already made plans with the owner for the use of this room. The owner showed them the room that was already prepared for use so that they could gather that very evening.

Although verses 14 and 16 sound as though the Passover meal is next in view, John's Gospel clearly shows that it was still twenty-four hours away (John 13:29; 18:28; 19:14, 31). It is best to interpret Mark as meaning that the disciples made arrangements for the week-long use of the room, although the actual Passover meal was still one day away.[2]

During the course of this last supper, Jesus announced His betrayal by one of those eating at the same table. He was fully aware of Judas's action. This seemed incredible to the disciples, and they asked (literally), "It isn't I, is it?" Apparently they all asked, even including Judas who wanted to escape detection (v. 19). The precise identification was made known only to John and Peter (John 13:23–26) and to Judas himself (Matt. 26:25).

Jesus explained that His betrayal was the fulfillment of Old Testament Scripture (Ps. 41:9). That this event had been prophesied and thus was certain to come to pass did not in any way lessen Judas' guilt. In view of the future punishment awaiting him, it would have been preferable if Judas had never been born. It is clear that Jesus knew exactly what Judas was doing. If Jesus had sought to escape from the plot, He could have done so; but He was willing to follow the plan of God as He accomplished the redemption of men.

This incident illustrates the biblical truths of divine sovereignty and human responsibility. What was happening was foreknown by God and had been announced by Him in Scripture hundreds of years before. Thus, it was certain of fulfillment. This is not a doctrine of fatalism, however, in which whatever will be, will be, so man has no personal responsibility. Scripture makes it clear that God holds man responsible for his actions. Even though we find it difficult

[2]The divergent chronological details between the Synoptic accounts and John force the interpreter either to explain the statements in John in the light of the Synoptic data, or vice versa. It is the view of this commentary that the interpreter should be guided by the many clear statements in John, which were written later than the Synoptics and perhaps with an attempt to clarify areas of confusion, rather than to force John into the supposed Synoptic pattern, or to conclude that a separate calendar was being used.

to reconcile these concepts, both are true and should be accepted because God's Word teaches them. We have a God who is "big enough" to grant man sufficient freedom to act without coercion and be morally responsible, and yet He knows exactly what we will do and has incorporated all as part of His plan.

During the meal Jesus instituted the symbols of His body and blood, which have been observed as ordinances by the Christian Church ever since. When He took the bread, prayed over it, and broke it for distribution, He said, "Take it; this is My body" (v. 22). It certainly seems clear that He was speaking metaphorically, inasmuch as His literal body was in the same room, but separate from the bread. He meant, "This bread represents My body." A similar action was taken with the cup, which He identified as symbolic of "My blood of the covenant" (v. 24). This was a reference to the new covenant that God had promised in Jeremiah 31:31–34, which would bring about an internal change ("I will put My law within them, and on their heart I will write it") and complete removal of guilt with no need of further sacrifice ("I will forgive their iniquity, and their sin I will remember no more"). The death of Jesus Christ upon the cross would provide the blood to validate that promised new covenant, and it was to be commemorated with the symbols of the bread and the cup by believers as a remembrance of Him (Luke 22:19). By this time Judas had already left (John 13:27–30).

The statement of Jesus that He would "never again drink of the fruit of the vine until that day…in the kingdom of God" (v. 25) makes it clear that His death would be very soon, apparently before another meal. Shortly thereafter, the group sang a hymn, probably a psalm, and retired to the Mount of Olives. This had been their custom during the past several days; they had made no provision for lodging within the city.

## Prediction of the Disciples' Failure, 14:27–31

Mark indicates that when the group left the Upper Room and made the short trip to the Mount of Olives, Jesus predicted that all of them would desert Him. He quoted Zechariah 13:7, which speaks of Messiah's followers who are scattered like sheep when their leader is smitten. He then applied this to the whole company of His disciples. Carrying on the figure of the shepherd going before his sheep, He pointed to the great reunion in Galilee that would follow His resurrection. This may refer to the time when He appeared to more than 500 at one time (1 Cor. 15:6). No mention is made of earlier post-resurrection appearances in Jerusalem.

Peter protested that he would stand true, even if all the rest would stumble. This statement is an assertion that Peter knew himself better than Christ did, and that he was more steadfast than the others. Jesus replied that he would not only fail along with the others, but it would occur that very night. Although cockcrowing was a common designation for a certain period of the night (cf. 13:35, 3:00 a.m.), the mention of a cock crowing "twice" points to the activity of some individual rooster (see 14:72).

## Events in Gethsemane, 14:32–42

On the slopes of the Mount of Olives was a garden called Gethsemane. The name means "oil press." There probably was an oil press in the garden. Directing eight of the disciples to stay in a certain spot and pray, Jesus took Peter, James, and John farther into the garden. These three had been granted special experiences on two other occasions (the raising of Jairus' daughter, 5:35–43; the Transfiguration, 9:28).

Admitting to the three that He was experiencing great trouble of soul, Jesus asked them to "remain here and keep watch" (v. 34). This should have reminded them of the recently given parable (Mark 13:35–37), in which they had been told to watch during the absence of the Master. He wanted them to be spiritually alert and to support Him with their prayers.

Jesus then withdrew a bit and prostrated Himself in prayer. The full depth of meaning of this prayer has never been plumbed by man. We can only suggest something of what we understand to have been involved. He prayed that if it were possible, the hour might pass from Him. He referred to the hour of His Passion, which would bring about His separation from God as He became man's sin-bearer. To feel the full sting of death was an experience to be dreaded, and Jesus asked that if there were some other way consistent with God's will, it might be done. The "cup" was an Old Testament symbol of the wrath of God (Ps. 75:8), and because He faced the prospect of bearing the penalty for sinful men, He naturally shrank from what it involved. However, in all of His asking, there was always perfect submission to the divine will and purpose. Such expressions as "if it were possible" (v. 35) and "not what I will, but what Thou wilt" (v. 36) make it clear that there was no desire whatsoever to take some path contrary to what the Father wished.

Instead of praying, however, the disciples had fallen asleep. Peter was singled out by Jesus, doubtless because he had claimed a strength superior to that of the others. The rebuke was not for sleeping or grieving but for failure to watch even for such a brief time.

Jesus pointed out the need for spiritual alertness because of the presence of temptation. Even though man's higher self enlightened by God (that is, the spirit) may desire to perform God's will, the old natural self (the flesh, or what man is unaided by God) is weak and will frustrate the accomplishment of the will of God. Praying is one way to maintain spiritual alertness. Yet, three times the disciples allowed the flesh to overpower them. At least they had the good sense to keep quiet and not offer excuses (v. 40).

"Arise, let us be going" (v. 42) was not an order to flee but to join the other eight disciples and meet Judas and the soldiers.

## The Arrest, 14:43–52

As Jesus was speaking to the disciples, Judas approached with a band of militia under orders from the Sanhedrin. John's Gospel tells us there were also Roman soldiers present (John 18:3). Judas led the way and gave the prearranged signal by kissing Jesus. He had not expected Jesus to step forward, and in the shadows of the garden some sign might be helpful to the soldiers who did not know Jesus.

Someone drew a sword and severed the ear of the high priest's servant. Only John's Gospel identifies the swordsman as Peter and the victim as a man named Malchus (John 18:10). Only Luke records the miracle of healing (Luke 22:51). Perhaps the Gospels of Matthew, Mark, and Luke were written early enough that some reprisals might have been provoked by unbelieving Jewish authorities against Peter and his family. When John's Gospel was written (A.D. 90), Peter was already dead.

Jesus asked His captors why they had come against Him as though He were an armed robber. During the past few days He had been teaching publicly in the temple, and no one had touched Him. It was clear that popular favor was with Jesus. Even now, He said, they could have no success in arresting Him by mere physical force. It was only because it was part of God's plan as given in prophecy that God allowed it. At this point Peter and all the others fled the scene, fulfilling another prediction of Jesus' earlier in the evening (v. 27).

Mark is the only Gospel to record the incident of verses 51 and 52 about a young man who was following Him. Since the story does not really figure very much in the whole narrative, the most plausible suggestion is that the man was Mark himself, who has in this unobtrusive way included himself in his account. Apparently the young man, whoever he was, had been roused from sleep and had hastily grabbed a sheet and followed. It is possible that the upper room where Jesus had been with the Twelve earlier in the evening was the home of Mark's mother. At least that home was an initial meeting place of the early Christians in Jerusalem (Acts 12:12). Perhaps Mark had wakened when Jesus and the disciples left for the Mount of Olives and had followed them. When the soldiers arrested Jesus, eleven disciples had escaped, but this young man was seized by the militia. He got loose by leaving behind the linen sheet and fleeing naked. In times of great fear or danger, proprieties may be overlooked. The naked human body was often seen in slaves, and the incident was probably not as shocking as it would be in our Western culture. (The term "naked" sometimes describes one clad in only an undergarment, however.)

## The Jewish Trials, 14:53–65

There were actually two sets of trials that Jesus had to face, both Jewish and Roman, and each set consisted of three phases. John's Gospel is the only one to describe the first phase in which Jesus was taken before Annas, the father-in-law of the present high priest Caiaphas (John 18:13–24). Although Annas had been deposed by the Romans some years before, he was held in high regard by the Jews and had much influence. He apparently lived in the same house as Caiaphas, since Peter's experiences seem to be in the same courtyard during the first two phases of the Jewish trials.

Mark describes the second phase of the Jewish night trial, this one before the Sanhedrin, composed of priests, elders, and scribes, under the chairmanship of the high priest Caiaphas. Peter, who had fled with all the other disciples, had come back to see what was going on, and was able to gain admittance to the courtyard through the intervention of "another disciple" (perhaps John himself) who was known by the high priest (John 18:15–16). He sat by the fire with some of the temple militia, warming himself on this chilly

Fig. 16. Gallicantu Church (left) and House of Caiaphas (right), sites of the Jewish trials of Jesus and the denials by Peter.

evening (v. 54). He was clearly afraid but still wanted to be near.

As the trial proceeded, efforts were made to obtain legal testimony against Jesus to support a charge. The mention of "the whole Council" (v. 55) shows that this was not just a few Sanhedrin members but virtually the entire group. Apparently there was no dearth of witnesses who were willing to perjure themselves. However, no two of them gave identical testimony on any point, so their testimony did not constitute a valid charge for conviction (see Deut. 17:6, 19:15).

The nearest His accusers could come to establishing a charge was when several (Matthew says there were two, 26:60–62) accused Jesus of claiming that He would destroy the temple and rebuild it after three days. This was a perversion of what Jesus had said three years before (John 2:19). At that time He had said, "Destroy this temple," which implies that they would destroy the temple. Furthermore, He was speaking of His own physical body, not the Jewish temple. The Jews of that time had an almost superstitious reverence for the temple, and this accusation suggested that Jesus was claiming some sort of magical powers to cause the temple to disappear and then to be replaced supernaturally. (In actuality, Jesus was predicting His own death and resurrection. Since He was the God-Man, His body was the true dwelling of God on earth, and in this sense His body was a "temple.") Yet even these false witnesses could not agree in sufficient detail to make the charge a valid one.

At this point the high priest himself took over the questioning and addressed Jesus directly. He wanted Jesus to say something, perhaps to incriminate Himself, since the testimony so far had been inconclusive. A defendant, however, could not be forced to testify against himself, so

Jesus kept silent. There was nothing He could explain that would really clarify anything. The charges were all trumped up, and even these were not legally supported with valid evidence. The wisest and most dignified course to follow was to make no comment at all unless some specific and supported charges were made. This had not yet been done.

The high priest persisted, however, and asked Jesus the direct question, "Are you the Christ, the Son of the Blessed One?" We should notice in this question that the high priest associated the idea of deity ("Son of the Blessed One") with messiahship ("Christ"). To answer such a question affirmatively was blasphemy in the thinking of any Jew who rejected Jesus. Although our Lord had refused to comment on the various wild charges thrown against Him, when He was asked the direct question, He responded with equal directness. After claiming deity and messiahship, He quoted from Daniel 7:13. Now as the Son of Man, He would soon be at God's right hand and would someday come in judgment.[3]

Caiaphas responded with the traditional gesture of abhorrence for blasphemy. A priest was not allowed to rend his garments for his personal problems (Lev. 21:10), but it was done for official acts (2 Kings 18:37). In the eyes of Caiaphas, Jesus incriminated Himself by His confession. Legally, a separate session was necessary at least one day later before final condemnation could be pronounced, but this was not observed. The Sanhedrin formally condemned

---

[3]When Jesus said that Caiaphas and the others would "see the Son of Man ...coming with the clouds of heaven," it may be wondered when this might be, inasmuch as unbelievers would not see Him at the Rapture, nor would they be raised at the Glorious Appearing when He comes to establish the Millennium. It is probably best to understand Jesus' use of the Daniel quotation to refer not only to the return in glory but also to the sitting at the right hand of Power. Thus all unbelievers will ultimately stand before Christ as the Divine Judge.

Jesus to death for blasphemy. The vote was unanimous; although doubtless a few were absent (Nicodemus, Joseph of Arimathaea). These formalities were followed by violence directed against Jesus, with the Sanhedrin members leading the abuse before they turned Him over to the temple police ("officers," v. 65b).

## Peter's Denials, 14:66–72

The trial must have been held in a room on a higher level than the courtyard outside. Mark introduced the mention of Peter at verse 54, so that readers might understand that what was happening in the courtyard was simultaneous with the trial going on before the Sanhedrin. While Peter was at the fire, a servant girl approached him and pointed him out as a companion of Jesus. Perhaps she was the same one who had let Peter in (John 18:17). Peter denied it, saying he did not know Jesus and did not understand what she was talking about. Leaving the fire, he then went to the porch, and at that time a cock crowed.[4] This should have caused Peter to stop his course of denials, but it did not.

The second denial occurred after a discussion among several bystanders. Mark indicates that the same girl was involved as in the previous encounter. Matthew mentions "another maid" (Matt. 26:71). Luke refers to another person (masculine, Luke 22:58). It appears that these people were

---

[4]The words "and a rooster crowed" appear in v. 68 (KJV) but are omitted by NASB and NIV on documentary evidence. It must be admitted the early manuscript support for their inclusion is not as strong as could be wished. However, the UBS Greek text in its fourth revised edition includes them in brackets with a C rating, which is a higher rating than in the previous edition. Inclusion of the words certainly fits the context well, inasmuch as there must have been a first cockcrowing before one could call another one a second (v. 72).

talking it over among themselves until finally one of them actually put the question to Peter. Once more Peter denied the relationship, and the term in v. 70 should be understood from the tense employed as "was repeatedly denying." He kept insisting that he was no disciple of Jesus.

The third denial followed an accusation from the bystanders that Peter's Galilean brogue revealed him to be a stranger in Jerusalem, just as Jesus was (see Matt. 26:73). All of the Twelve were Galileans except Judas Iscariot. This time Peter denied with the greatest vehemence, calling down anathemas upon his own head if he were lying ("to curse") and invoking God as witness to his veracity ("to swear"). Immediately a second crowing of the cock struck home to Peter, and he left to consider[5] with many tears the enormity of what he had done.

## Truths to Remember

• In spite of man's aspirations, he is doomed to fail ultimately if he does not rely upon God's strength. "The flesh is weak" (v. 38).

• Even though Jesus is the Son of God, He knows from experience what it means to go through deep mental and spiritual anguish.

• Prayer is the great safeguard against temptation. One does not fall into sin while engaged in genuine prayer.

---

[5] In verse 72 the Greek phrase *epibalōn eklaien*, particularly the first word, is very difficult to translate. Bauer-Arndt-Gingrich have an extended discussion of it and state that its meaning here in Mark remains in doubt (290). I would propose the sense, "having put [his mind] upon [it], he began weeping."

# Part IV

## The Death and Resurrection

### Mark 15:1–16:20

# 15

# THE DEATH OF CHRIST
## Mark 15:1–47

The Christian faith is based upon historical facts, not mere philosophy. Christianity exists because at a given point in time certain events happened. God sent His only Son into the world at a certain time and in a certain place. The history of this remarkable event is chronicled for us most completely in the four Gospels. The high point of Christ's experience on earth was the closing week, when the redemptive purpose for which He came was accomplished. The importance that the Gospel writers attached to the consummation of His career may be seen in the proportion of space allotted to it in each Gospel. Mark devotes six of his sixteen chapters to the final week.

It should also be noted, however, that all of the Gospel writers resist any effort to "theologize" regarding the Crucifixion and its aftermath. Even though the Gospels were probably written later than some of the Epistles (certainly John's Gospel was), and the Church that received them must have been well aware of Paul's teaching regarding the believer's identification with Christ in His death and resurrection (Rom. 6:3–13, Col. 2:12), not one of the Gospels tries to make this point. Each one sticks to the historical facts involved. Consequently, we have confidence that the biblical record is reliable. It is in no sense a mere subjective interpretation of a few facts produced by devotees of a religious system, but an authentic record of what actually happened, preserved for us in four largely independent accounts that we might know the certainty of those things in which we have been instructed (see Luke 1:4).

## The Roman Trial, 15:1–15

### The Questioning, 15:1–5

Very early the next morning the Jews held a second meeting of the Sanhedrin. It may have been an attempt at legality, even though the law was still being flouted because these were not a full day apart.[1] "Held a consultation" (v. 1) may imply "reached a decision" (NIV). The Jewish trials had concluded that Jesus was guilty of blasphemy and thus merited death. Mark uses this phase of the Jewish religious proceedings as a bridge to the Roman trials as he moves immediately to describe what happened with the Roman authorities. The Romans reserved to themselves the right to authorize all capital punishment cases. Therefore it was necessary for Jesus to be transported to the headquarters of the Roman governor, Pontius Pilate. Fortunately for the Jews, Pilate happened to be in Jerusalem at this time. His usual residence was in Caesarea.

Although this was a most early hour for the Roman governor to be approached about a judicial matter, it must not be forgotten that Pilate doubtless had been forewarned by the Jews that he would be needed. It must have been Pilate who authorized the detachment of Roman soldiers to take part in the arrest of Jesus (John 18:12).

---

[1]Not all agree on this understanding of the text. Lane, for example, explains this reference as simply the conclusion of the meeting of the Sanhedrin, which had occurred around midnight. *Mark* in *NICNT* series (Grand Rapids: Eerdmans, 1974), 545, ftn. 1.

The Jews must have told Pilate that Jesus was a dangerous political figure, for his first question to Jesus was, "Are You the King of the Jews?" The Jewish leaders probably knew that the political overtones of this accusation would appear much more serious to Pilate than the real charge of blasphemy. They hoped that Pilate would ratify their verdict without much further investigation. Jesus readily admitted He was the King of the Jews. Yet Pilate does not seem to be greatly alarmed by the admission. Because of this, the Jews added many other charges against Jesus. They are listed in Luke 23:1–2. These additional accusations were not answered by our Lord. Pilate was surprised that Jesus offered no defense, but he did not conclude that silence meant guilt. Of course, he should not have allowed unsupported accusations to be made. All legal charges should be accompanied by evidence and witnesses. None of these were presented by the Jews. It can hardly be doubted that Pilate was impressed by the dignified bearing of his prisoner, and he must have wondered why the Jews were so fanatical in their hatred of Him.[2]

**The Counter Offer, 15:6–11**

It had been customary at this great national feast for the Roman governor to release one Jewish prisoner as a gesture of good will. At that very time there were in prison a group of insurrectionists and their leader, Barabbas.

Mark seems to suggest that the initiative for the release of one prisoner lay with the people, but Matthew indicates that Pilate himself suggested it (Matt. 2:17). Because it is

[2]At this point in the proceedings, Pilate sent Jesus to Herod Antipas for the second phase of the Roman trials (Luke 23:6–12). Jesus, however, made no answer to Herod's questioning, so He was sent back to Pilate for the third phase of the trials.

difficult to find any clear motive for the people at this point in the narrative, it is best to understand that Pilate suggested it as a way to release Jesus, and then the people began to beg him to follow through with the policy. Pilate naively thought that if the people were given a choice between the release of the vicious Barabbas and Jesus, they would surely choose Jesus. How badly he misjudged his crowd.

Pilate seemed genuinely puzzled that the Jewish authorities would prefer Barabbas. He must have known when he was appointed by Rome to the governorship that he was going to a nation that was profoundly religious. Yet, he had soon learned that their religious practice did not ensure spirituality, and they could play politics in the most murderous fashion. Through his advisors, he had learned that the problem with Jesus as far as the Jewish leaders were concerned was one of envy (v. 10).

Where were the voices of those who shouted Christ's praises at the triumphal entry? Why did no one come to His defense? Verse 11 explains that the chief priests stirred up this particular crowd to demand Barabbas rather than Jesus. Events had happened so rapidly since the arrest the night before that it is quite possible most of Jesus' friends in the city didn't know what was happening until the crucifixion was under way. This crowd at the trial could well have been bribed to shout as they did.

If the people had chosen Jesus instead of Barabbas, Pilate could have upheld the Sanhedrin's verdict of guilt and then granted Jesus a release. Thus, he would have satisfied his own conscience regarding this innocent man. But the people did not come to his aid, and he was too weak to stand up for the right against the clamor of the Jewish leaders.

## The Sentencing, 15:12–15

Having chosen Barabbas as the one they desired to be released, the Jews were now asked what they wanted done with Jesus. Perhaps Pilate could hardly believe they would really demand the death penalty. But the crowd had been thoroughly persuaded by its leaders and cried, "Crucify him!"

Pilate's sense of Roman justice was amazed at this obstinate and emotional demand for the blood of an innocent man. He was convinced that no crime had been committed and that the only real problem was internal Jewish strife. Religious issues may cause feelings to run deep, but here was hardly a matter for which Roman law could support an execution. The crowd, however, was not interested in conducting a rational discussion. They continued to cry, "Crucify him!"

The tragedy of Pilate was his lack of moral courage. He knew very well what was right. John's Gospel records him as saying at least three times that Jesus was innocent of any crime (John 18:38; 19:4, 6). It is bad enough to lack the moral perception to know what is right. But when one knows what is right and does not act in accordance with it, his case is infinitely worse.

Moved by the desire to satisfy the Jewish authorities, Pilate released Barabbas and ordered Jesus to be crucified. Perhaps he was afraid his superiors in Rome would censure him if he aroused the displeasure of the nation.

Before the order for crucifixion was given, Pilate arranged for Jesus to be scourged. This was an exceptionally cruel punishment in which the victim's back was laid bare and he was lashed with a whip consisting of strips of leather imbedded with pieces of metal or bone. It was commonly done as a prelude to execution, and sometimes prisoners died from the scourging alone. It was considered so cruel that Roman citizens were exempted from it. John's Gospel shows that this scourging was actually done at Pilate's order with the hope of securing sympathy for Jesus and perhaps even yet bringing about His release (19:1–5). This did not happen, however, so the order was given for execution.

## The Soldiers Mockery, 15:16–19

"And the soldiers led him away inside the courtyard, which is the Praetorium" is a literal translation of verse 16. Because the Jews had refused to enter the Gentile headquarters of Pilate (John 18:28), it had been necessary for Pilate to conduct much of the trial outside. Now that the trial was over and a sentence had been pronounced, Jesus was turned over to the soldiers for execution. They took Him into the inner courtyard[3] and summoned all the available soldiers for a brief time of outrageous sport before crucifixion.

The idea that Jesus claimed to be "King of the Jews" caught the fancy of these rough soldiers. They placed a purple robe around his shoulders. It was probably a faded soldier's cloak, used here to represent royal purple (Matthew calls it "scarlet," 27:28). They fashioned a crude crown from

[3]The actual location of the Praetorium remains a matter of debate. Some insist that Pilate, whose residence was in Caesarea, normally stayed at Herod's Palace when he came to Jerusalem. However, the fact that Herod himself was in Jerusalem at this feast time, and that he and Pilate were previously estranged (Luke 23:12), would make it more likely that he would have stayed at the fortress Antonia, adjacent to the temple mount. Discussion of the evidence for both views is found in Jack Finegan, *The Archaeology of the New Testament* (Princeton, 1969), 156–158.

a thorn branch (perhaps a thorn bush grew in the courtyard), and pressed it on His brow. Then they pretended to pay homage to Him, saying, "Hail, King of the Jews!" As each one approached Him, he would strike Him on the head with a reed, perhaps one that had been placed in Jesus' hand for a scepter (Matt. 27:29). This would drive the thorns into His brow even deeper. Spitting is one of the most humiliating insults, and this was coupled with a genuflecting that was pure mockery.

## The Crucifixion, 15:20–41

### Preparations, 15:20–23

When the mocking was finished, Jesus' own clothes were put back on Him and He was led away for execution. The place of crucifixion was outside the city walls.

Because of the tortures Jesus had endured, He needed help to drag His cross through the city streets. Therefore, the soldiers commandeered a Cyrenian Jew, who was just entering the city, to perform this task. Mark identified this man, Simon, as the father of Alexander and Rufus. The only way such an identification would have been helpful was if these sons were known to Mark's readers. Inasmuch as the Gospel was originally written for readers in Rome, it is possible that this Rufus was the Roman Christian mentioned by Paul in Romans 16:13.

As Jesus was made ready for crucifixion, the soldiers offered Him a drugged wine, commonly provided to make the victims more docile. It is said that pious women from Jerusalem regularly furnished such for the prisoners. Jesus, however, did not want His faculties to be clouded, so He refused the potion.

223

The place of execution was called Golgotha, which means "Place of a Skull." It must have been so named for its topography as a round-topped hill. The suggestion that the name came from skulls lying around from previous executions is unlikely, for Jews always buried them.

### The First Three Hours, 15:24–32

Mark and the other evangelists describe the Crucifixion in the simplest of terms. We know from Jesus' statement later that nails were driven into His hands (John 20:27). Victims often lingered for several days, dying finally from thirst, exposure, and exhaustion.

The third hour by Jewish reckoning corresponds to 9 a.m. During the first three hours Jesus was on the cross, the soldiers divided His clothes among themselves. The action of gambling for the prisoner's clothing was a common practice of soldiers, but here it was also a fulfillment of Psalm 22:18. Of course, the soldiers were unaware of any prophecy being fulfilled.

Mark's mention of the "third hour" (v. 25) seems in conflict with John's statement of the "sixth hour" (John 19:14) when Pilate sentenced Jesus. If John was using Jewish time reckoning, it would mean that Jesus was not even sentenced until noon. If Roman reckoning was used, it would indicate 6:00 a.m., a three hour discrepancy. The best solution (in my view) is to regard Pilate's sentencing to have occurred early in the morning, sometime after 6:00 a.m., and the Crucifixion to have been fully accomplished by 9:00 a.m.

Over the cross was a placard identifying the prisoner and stating the charge against him. In the case of Jesus, it was more of a title than an accusation. Although the four Gospels record the wording of this title in slightly varying fashion, there is no contradiction. Mark's is the most condensed of the four. (The title appeared in three languages, which may also be a factor in the variation.)

Two others were crucified with Jesus, one on each side. They were probably the associates of Barabbas, with Jesus occupying the central cross that had been intended for the leader of the band. The same word for "robber" which is used for them is also used for Barabbas in John 18:40.

Verse 28 does not appear in the best manuscripts. Perhaps it was picked up from Luke 22:37 by a copyist.

The outcries of those who said He had promised to destroy the temple and rebuild it in three days picked up the same accusation used in Jewish trials. Perhaps they had been present at that time. Of course, the accusation was a complete distortion of what Jesus had said and clearly missed the point He was making (see John 2:19–22). The shout of the people, "Save yourself!" suggests what these people would have done if they had been in Jesus' place. Most of us are concerned with ourselves first of all. These people just could not comprehend how Jesus could let Himself be killed if He really was able to prevent it. Their attitude was He had made great claims, but He couldn't even take care of Himself.

The remarks of the priests and scribes (vv. 31–32) seem to have been made to one another, rather than shouted at Jesus. Yet, they descended to the same low level as the populace. When they said, "He saved others," they were speaking with irony. They certainly did not believe that Jesus had saved others. What they meant was that since He seemed powerless to save Himself from the cross, He really couldn't have saved anyone else either. Yet there was truth in what they said, even though it was not the sense in which they meant it. In order to save others, Jesus could not save Himself. He had to go to the cross as our sin-bearer if He was to provide salvation in the fullest sense.

The priests said that if Jesus would demonstrate His power by coming down from the cross, they would believe Him. This shows their misunderstanding of what it means to believe. Faith that demands seeing first is no faith at all. Even the two robbers joined in reviling Jesus. Mark does not record that one of them later repented (see Luke 23:39–43).

### The Last Three Hours, 15:33–38

Mark continues to state the time of day in accord with Jewish reckoning. The period from the sixth to the ninth hour means noon to 3:00 p.m. The darkness that enveloped the land at this time was certainly supernaturally timed to coincide with the period in which Jesus experienced the spiritual darkness of separation from God as our sin-bearer. It was probably also supernaturally caused, inasmuch as there could not have been a natural eclipse of the sun at full moon (Passover occurred at full moon each year). Whether the darkness was over the whole globe or merely over the land (that is, Jerusalem or Palestine) is not certain from the text. No records exist of this event outside of Scripture. The unusual darkness is reminiscent of the plague of darkness for three days in Egypt, which pictured God's judgment of that nation (Ex. 10:21–23).

Just before His death Jesus made a loud outcry. The words are given in Aramaic, the native tongue of Palestine that Jesus normally used. He was quoting Psalm 22:1. "My God, my God, why hast thou forsaken me?" is one of the most profound statements in Scripture. This is the only one of Christ's sayings from the cross that Mark records. Coming as it did from the lips of the Son of God, it must have meant more than simply a feeling of loneliness. No explanation is adequate except that this was God's judicial abandonment of the Son as our sin-bearer. Now Jesus was experiencing the wrath of God by being separated from Him for three hours. Jesus endured spiritual death (that is, separation from God) as well as physical death in our place. We can hardly begin to imagine what this meant to the Holy Son of God, whose fellowship with the Father had always been perfect and unbroken.

Some of the bystanders thought that Jesus was calling for the aid of Elijah. Perhaps they misunderstood the words (the opening words were similar in sound to the name "Elijah") or else they were making a sort of pun. Because Elijah was supposed to come in connection with Messiah, they suggested that perhaps He was asking Elijah to rescue Him and enable Him to fulfill His messianic claims.

Jesus was given a sponge of vinegar, or sour wine, and because this was not a drugged potion, He did not refuse it. It may have been given to ease His thirst a bit and thus prolong His life to see whether Elijah really would come. The soldiers would not be unwilling to allow this brief prolongation of life, for this was one of the tortures of crucifixion.

Mark describes the moment of Christ's death by noting that He "uttered a loud cry, and breathed His last" (v. 37). Only Luke (23:46) and John (19:30) record the content of His outcry.

Mark, along with Matthew and Luke, mentions the remarkable tearing of the veil in the temple (v. 38). The term used was often used to denote the curtain that hung between the holy place and the holy of holies. It split in two from top to bottom, thus exposing to view the innermost chamber of the sanctuary. Whether this was physically possible as a result of the earthquake (Matt. 27:51) is debated. Even if the earthquake were the providential cause, its timing was certainly supernatural. The tearing of the veil symbolized the removal of the barrier to the presence of God through the atoning death of Christ. (See Heb. 9:7–12 and 10:19–22, where this symbolism is applied.) This splitting of the temple curtain is not reported in any non-biblical Jewish writings. If it was observed only by the priests who then repaired it without public announcement, it could have been reported to the Church by priests who were later converted (Acts 6:7).[4]

## The Spectators, 15:39–41

In addition to the priests and other bystanders already mentioned in Mark's account, there were others present. Special reference is made to the comment by the Roman centurion. He was the officer in charge of the detachment of soldiers who had carried out the crucifixion. Clearly impressed by Jesus and all that had transpired, he said, "Truly this man was the Son of God." Just how much he meant by his use of this term is disputed. He was a Roman, and pagan ideas could have been involved. On the other hand, if the one malefactor could learn enough while on the cross to put his faith in Christ (Luke 23:39–43), why could not the centurion have done likewise?

Also at the scene were some faithful women who had assisted in the support of Jesus during His ministry. Mary

[4]Lane, however, seems more favorable to the view that the veil in question is the one between the outer courts and the holy place. Otherwise, it would have been unobserved by non-priests and could not serve as a public sign. William L. Lane, *The Gospel According to Mark* (Grand Rapids: Eerdmans, 1974), 574–575. None of the Synoptics, however, imply that this was a public occurrence that created any widespread notice.

Magdalene had been rescued from demon possession (Luke 8:2). The other Mary may have been the mother of an apostle, James of Alphaeus.[5] Salome was the wife of Zebedee (Matt. 27:56) and the mother of two apostles. She may also have been the sister of Mary, Jesus' mother (see the parallel passage in John 19:25, where Salome seems to be the proper name of the woman who is merely mentioned as "His mother's sister").

## The Burial, 15:42–47

The Jews sometimes spoke of a "first evening" to denote the period between mid-afternoon and sundown. That is what Mark means when he says that evening had come. It was nearly sundown, when the Passover Feast Sabbath would begin.

Joseph of Arimathaea, a Sanhedrin member who is not known to us prior to this incident, asked Pilate for the corpse of Jesus. He was a godly Jew who looked for the messianic kingdom, but until this moment he had not openly identified himself with Jesus although he had been a disciple (Matt. 27:57; John 19:38). Since he was not a relative, he ran the risk of social disapproval by asking for the body of an executed victim. Pilate was surprised that Jesus had died so quickly. When the centurion verified that Jesus was dead, permission was granted. Joseph then obtained a linen cloth, and, after wrapping Jesus' body in it, he placed it in

---

[5]James the Less (Mark 15:40) may be the same person as James of Alphaeus, who is named in all the lists of the apostles (Matt. 10:3; Mark 3:18; Luke 6:15; Acts 1:13). If so, his mother Mary was the wife of Alphaeus, who may also have had the name Clopas (John 19:25); or, this Mary could have been the daughter of a man named Clopas.

his own rock-hewn tomb nearby (only Matthew records that Joseph was the owner of this tomb, 27:60). The two Marys observed the proceedings. They were among those who later prepared spices for anointing the body. But they would have no occasion to use them, for Jesus had risen.

Fig. 17. Stone of Unction in the Church of the Holy Sepulchre, traditional place where Jesus was taken down from the cross and anointed for burial.

## Truths to Remember

• The Roman trial, part of the greatest judicial system in the world of Jesus' day, revealed absolutely no guilt in Jesus.

• Jesus was for three hours forsaken by the Father so that believers would never need to be.

• The blood of Christ offered at Calvary provided permanent access for believers to the actual presence of God, as symbolized by the temple court.

# 16

# THE RESURRECTION OF CHRIST
## Mark 16:1–20

The Resurrection is crucial to the Christian faith. Some people today try to avoid this fact. Because miracles in the Bible are an embarrassment to those who reject the supernatural claims of Scripture and yet think of themselves as Christians, they try to explain away the Resurrection. Explanations range from outright denial to assertions that it doesn't really matter. What is important, it is claimed, is the teaching He left, or His example, or the principles for which He died. One school of critics does away with the historical validity of the Resurrection by claiming that the Gospel records are merely a reflection of the way the Church theorized about Jesus many years later and are not to be thought of as records of historical facts.

The Gospels, however, present the Resurrection as a historical fact. And when the Gospels were written, many people were still living who had known Jesus and had been witnesses of His post-Resurrection appearances. If the Gospels were inaccurate, it would have been noticed at once.

The Resurrection transformed the disciples from dejected, fearful, uncertain men to dedicated, courageous, and effective witnesses for their Lord.

The resurrection was the prominent feature of the earliest apostolic preaching (Acts 1:22; 2:22–36; 3:15; 4:10; 5:30–32). These men were utterly convinced that Jesus had risen physically from the tomb, and they were willing to spend their lives in carrying out the commands that He had given them. The Gospels are the records that were given to the Church by God, using the human authority of the apostles. What we read in them about the Resurrection is what the apostolic eyewitnesses reported.

The Epistles reveal that the Resurrection is more than merely a proof of the deity of Christ. To be sure it was the greatest sign of His messiahship (John 2:19–22, Matt. 12:38–40). But Peter, for example, taught that we are "born again to a living hope through the resurrection of Jesus Christ from the dead" (1 Peter 1:3). Paul said that "if Christ has not been raised, your faith is worthless; you are still in your sins" (1 Cor. 15:17). The Resurrection is vitally involved in man's salvation, for salvation comes as we are identified with Christ in His death and in His resurrection. God sees believers as dying with His Son and also as sharing in His resurrection life (Rom. 6:1–4). If He were still dead, He would still be paying the penalty for sin, and thus a completed salvation could not be offered to men.

## The Angelic Announcement, 16:1–8

When the Sabbath was over, three women (previously named in 15:40, 47) bought spices to anoint Jesus' body. Because the Jewish day ended at sundown, it is commonly explained that this occurred on Saturday night at the close of the weekly Sabbath. However, this hardly provides enough time for the work of preparing the spices into ointment. Furthermore, to make this purchase of the spices harmonize with Luke 23:53–56, one must understand that the spices were bought before the weekly Sabbath, not after. The best harmonization is provided by understanding that the Crucifixion occurred before the Passover Sabbath, and that there was a day between the Passover Sabbath and the weekly Sabbath that year. This gives us the following chronology: Wednesday, Crucifixion; Thursday, Passover Feast Sabbath; Friday, purchase of spices by the women; Saturday, weekly Sabbath. This explanation also allows for a full three days and three nights in the tomb[1]—from sundown Wednesday night to sundown Saturday night, which was the beginning of the first day of the week by Jewish reckoning.

Fig. 18. The Garden Tomb, an early tomb in Jerusalem surrounded by a beautiful garden, similar to the place where Jesus was buried, and where He rose from the dead.

[1]Matthew 12:39–40. Although one may explain Friday evening to Sunday morning as parts of three days by Jewish reckoning, it is not so easy to equate this with "three days and three nights." The idea of a Wednesday crucifixion will probably never displace the traditional view of crucifixion on Good Friday, but the possibility is worth consideration.

Very early on Sunday morning this group of women went to the tomb. A comparison of all the Gospel accounts shows the need for some harmonization. It was still dark when they started out (John 20:1) but was daylight by the time they arrived (Mark 16:2). A study of John 20 in connection with Mark reveals that something like this must have happened: The group of women started out together (Mark 16:1–2). Mary Magdalene, however, must have gone on ahead and reached the tomb first. When she found it empty, she ran away to inform Peter and John without telling the other women (John 20:1–2). Meanwhile, the other women arrived.

As they neared the tomb, they began to wonder who would roll back the heavy stone that blocked the entrance to the sepulcher. These women had been so occupied with the task of preparing spices and with their grief that they had not considered the problem before. They seemed unaware that a guard had been posted and that the tomb was sealed by the governor's orders. In such tombs there was usually a huge, round stone placed in a sloping track. When the tomb was ready to be closed, the blocks would be removed and the stone would roll down the track into position before the door. It would take great effort to roll it back.

Their worries were needless, however, for as they came within sight of the tomb, they could see that the stone had already been rolled away. Mark does not tell how it happened, but Matthew reports that an angel rolled it back (28:2). Perhaps it fell flat so the angel could sit on it.

When the women entered the tomb, they saw a young man clothed in white (16:5). Matthew calls him an angel. Luke says there were two (24:4), but Mark mentions only the speaker who calmed them by explaining what had happened.

The popular notion that angels are winged females is without scriptural support. When they appear to humans, they appear as men. The women were dumbfounded. Things were utterly different from what they were expecting to find. John 20:5–7 indicates that the grave clothes were still lying there, but the body was absent.

The angel gave the women some instructions. They were to leave the tomb and report these things to the disciples. Peter was singled out for special mention (Mark 16:7). This was doubtless because of Peter's previous denials. He was to be assured that Christ had not cast him off. This special note should be a great comfort to believers in times of failure. The knowledge that our Lord still has an interest even in His erring children should increase our love for Him and should serve to strengthen us against future failure. Mark is the only Gospel to report this special mention to Peter, and the fact that Peter is probably the source of Mark's material makes this reference a poignant one.

The angel also informed the women about a special meeting of the resurrected Jesus with His disciples in Galilee. Actually, Jesus would appear to the disciples later that same day, while they were still in Jerusalem. The meeting in Galilee would be a bit later. Perhaps it was referred to in this way because it was the large gathering of more than 500, thus including more than just the Apostles (1 Cor. 15:6).

The women emerged from the cave-like tomb and fled the scene. The excitement produced by the past few moments caused a physical trembling after the first shock wore off. They reacted with fear to being in the presence of supernatural beings and events. We must understand Mark's statement that the women didn't say anything to anyone in harmony with the other Gospel accounts. Mark means they did not blurt out the news to everyone they met, but kept quiet until they had located the Apostles.

Mark has thus recorded for us the first authoritative explanation of the Resurrection. It was given by an angel to the women who had come to anoint the dead body of Jesus. How appropriate that those who had come to do Him honor even after death should be the first to learn that He had risen!

(The oldest manuscripts do not contain verses 9–20. For this reason, most modern English versions put them in brackets, or otherwise indicate that they are textually doubtful. However, this portion is so well known to Bible readers that it seems best to leave it in the text and simply indicate that the documentary support is not as strong as the rest of the text of Mark. For a discussion of this problem, see the section "Distinctive Features of Mark's Gospel" in chapter 1, pp. 6–8.)

## The Appearance to Mary Magdalene, 16:9–11

Although the news that Jesus had risen was reported first by the angel to the other women, the first actual appearance of the risen Christ was to Mary Magdalene. This woman is regarded by many as the foremost of Christ's female disciples. Her life had been rescued from demon possession when Jesus cast seven demons out from her. It is small wonder that she brought to our Lord the deepest gratitude and devotion. The popular idea that she had once been an immoral woman is based on the identification of her with the sinful woman who anointed Jesus' feet (Luke 7:36–50). Careful study of the Gospels reveals absolutely no connection, however, and thus it is unwarranted to accuse her of a particularly unsavory past, apart from the unfortunate experience of demon possession. A more complete account of the appearance to Mary Magdalene is found in John 20:11–18.

It seems that Mary, after going ahead of the other women and finding the tomb empty, went to report this fact to Peter and John (John 20:1–2). After the other women had gone to the tomb and left, and after Peter and John had done the same, Mary Magdalene must have returned to the sepulcher alone. It was here that Jesus appeared to her. She must have responded by touching Him, just as a group of women did a bit later (Matt. 28:9), for Jesus told her to stop clinging to Him (John 20:17). This confirmed the fact that this was an actual physical resurrection, not a vision or hallucination.

Returning to the other disciples, she found them still overpowered by grief. They had not believed the report of the other women. John, on the basis of the evidence he saw at the tomb, had come to the conclusion that Jesus was raised, but he was apparently not among those whom Mary contacted at this time (John 20:8). We should not conclude that the eleven were all in one spot until later in the day, and even then Thomas was absent. When Mary found some of the disciples, she announced that she had seen Jesus alive. Yet they did not believe her. Not to be believed when one is telling the truth is always a humiliating experience. On the other hand, the obstinate refusal of the disciples to believe without adequate proof does provide assurance for us that the evidence for the physical resurrection was compelling.

## The Appearance to Two in the Country, 16:12–13

A more complete account of Jesus' appearance to two disciples is found in Luke 24:13–35. Jesus joined two who were walking in the countryside. They were on the way to Emmaus, a village about seven miles from Jerusalem. One of the two was named Cleopas.

Mark says that Jesus appeared "in a different form" (v. 12). Luke says that "their eyes were prevented from recognizing Him" (Luke 24:16). Apparently, our Lord's resurrection body was capable of certain changes, and this is why they did not recognize Him at once. Perhaps this is also why Mary Magdalene mistook Jesus for the gardener when He first appeared to her (John 20:15).

There were certain practical advantages in having these two not recognize Jesus at once. In the Lukan account we learn that Jesus discussed certain matters with them, including the relevance of various Old Testament passages to Himself. If they had known that it was Jesus, they would have become so excited it is doubtful they could have listened carefully and thoughtfully to the import of what He was saying. Not until they were eating together did Jesus reveal Himself to them.

The two then returned to Jerusalem to inform the disciples of their experience. Here Mark seems to contradict Luke, for Luke says they were greeted with the words, "The Lord has really risen" (Luke 24:34), but Mark says that those in Jerusalem did not believe them. Yet, we must also note that even Luke's Gospel reports after this event that they "could not believe it for joy" (v. 41). Apparently, the rapidly unfolding events were too much for them, and what resulted was a perfectly understandable mixture of excitement, joy, and hesitancy to believe fully. Their real belief did not seem to develop until after Jesus Himself appeared to the disciples (Mark 16:14).

# The Appearance to the Eleven, 16:14–18

According to John 20:19, Jesus' first appearance to the disciples occurred on the evening of Resurrection Day. This was the occasion when Jesus showed them His hands and feet and invited them to touch Him (Luke 24:39–40). Thomas was not present at this gathering (John 20:24), although Mark calls them the eleven (Judas Iscariot, of course, was also not there). "The Eleven" was now apparently the official name of the group, even though there was at least one absentee.

As Jesus presented Himself to this group of His closest associates, He rebuked them for unbelief and hardheartedness. Thomas was not the only apostle to doubt. His doubt merely lasted longer than that of the others. The particular aspect of unbelief that Jesus denounced was the refusal to accept the testimony of those who had already seen the risen Savior. He did not mean they were unbelievers in the absolute sense, and were without salvation. But this failure to accept what Jesus had taught before the Crucifixion marked a spiritual lack on their part. If they had been spiritually alert, the words of the women and the two from Emmaus would have reminded them of what Jesus had specifically predicted about His Resurrection.

Jesus commissioned the apostles to proclaim the Gospel throughout all the world. Later, He assured them that power to accomplish this task would be provided by the Holy Spirit, who would be given in a new way at Pentecost (Acts 1:3–8). The importance of this proclamation was indicated by explaining the results that would come to those who heard it. Just two responses can be made to the Gospel. A hearer will either believe or fail to believe.

"He who has believed and has been baptized shall be saved" (v. 16). This verse is sometimes used by those who insist that water baptism is essential for salvation. Several factors should be noted in the statement. It is clear that both believing and being baptized are actions applying to the same person. Therefore, it seems that the person who believes will also undergo baptism. This should caution us against the notion that baptism in water is optional or unimportant. It is the consistent viewpoint of the New Testament that a Christian believer will be baptized. The idea of an unbaptized Christian is never assumed or presented in Scripture.

The second part of the statement should also be carefully noted. "He who has disbelieved shall be condemned." The basis for condemnation is unbelief (not lack of water baptism). Thus we conclude that the basis for salvation (that is, escape from condemnation) is belief. Baptism will then be an act of obedience by the saved person, not a rite to procure salvation.

Jesus promised that believers would be supernaturally empowered to display their new life and to authenticate their message as from God. The casting out of demons was frequently performed in the apostolic age (Acts 5:16; 16:16–18; 19:12). Speaking with new tongues occurred on the Day of Pentecost (Acts 2:4), at Caesarea (Acts 10:46), at Ephesus (Acts 19:6), and at Corinth (1 Cor. 12–14). Paul was miraculously delivered from a serpent's bite (Acts 28:3–6). There are no biblical instances of miraculous deliverance from the drinking of poison, although there is no reason to doubt that instances such as this did occur. There is absolutely no warrant for any voluntary handling of snakes or drinking of poisons, as some extreme sects have advocated.

## The Ascension, 16:19–20

From the reading of Mark alone one might conclude that the Ascension occurred on Resurrection Day, following the appearance to the Eleven in the upper room. However, a comparison of all the Gospel accounts, as well as Acts 1, indicates this was not the case. A period of forty days elapsed before the Ascension (Acts 1:3). During that time there were numerous appearances of the resurrected Lord to His followers. Included were the disciples' trip to Galilee, where Jesus met with them, and a return trip to Jerusalem. Both Luke (24:50) and Acts (1:12) indicate that the Ascension took place from the Mount of Olives in the vicinity of Bethany, just outside Jerusalem. Mark's account is greatly condensed, but it does not contradict the information supplied by the others.

After Jesus had given the disciples His final words, He was taken up into heaven. The various post-Resurrection appearances of Jesus seem to have been ended by a sudden vanishing from human sight, but that was not the case here. They were able to watch Jesus ascend (Acts 1:9–10), and this difference, coupled with the angelic explanation (Acts 1:11), indicated to them that this was the last time they would see Him until His Second Coming.

Mark's statement that Jesus "sat down at the right hand of God" is the only place in the Gospels where this is asserted. Of course, it is mentioned in Acts and the Epistles. It marked the completion of Christ's work in providing atonement and also indicated His position of authority with the Father.

The concluding verse of the Gospel summarizes the apostolic activity that followed. After waiting in Jerusalem until Pentecost, as Jesus had commanded (Acts 1:4), they began the various careers that carried the Gospel to all segments of the Roman world by the close of the first century. The Lord confirmed the spoken word of the apostles by the miracles that He empowered them to perform. By the end of the apostolic age, when the Word was completely written (that is, the New Testament), there was no need for continued confirmation by miracles; the age of apostolic miracles ceased. Whether we regard Mark's original conclusion as verse 8 or verse 20, the great "beginning of the gospel of Jesus Christ, the Son of God" (Mark 1:1) as preached by Peter has been recorded by Mark for the benefit of future generations as they in turn live out their Christian lives and seek to convey their witness to a needy world.

## Truths to Remember

• The disciples believed that Jesus had risen from the dead only when they received unmistakable proof.

• The only thing that prevents a person from being saved is failure to believe the gospel.

• The miracles that Jesus promised to the apostles were fulfilled by them, and there is no reason why we would expect them to continue in our day.

# BIBLIOGRAPHY

Aland, Barbara; Kurt Aland; Johannes Karavidopoulos; Carlo M. Martini; and Bruce Metzger. *The Greek New Testament,* 4th rev. ed. Stuttgart: Deutsche Bibelgesellschaft, 1993.

Aland, Kurt. *Synopsis Quattuor Evangeliorum.* Stuttgart: Deutsche Bibelstiflung Stuttgart, 1976.

Alexander, Joseph Addison. *The Gospel According to Mark.* London: Billing and Sons, n.d. Reprint edition: Banner of Truth.

Arndt, William F. and F. Wilbur Gingrich. *A Greek-English Lexicon of the New Testament.* 2nd ed. Chicago: University of Chicago Press, 1979.

*Baedeker Israel.* Translated by James Hogarth. New York: Macmillan Travel, 1995.

Brooks, James A. *Mark* in *The New American Commentary.* Nashville: Broadman, 1991.

Bruce, Alexander Balmain. "The Synoptic Gospels," *The Expositor's Greek Testament,* Vol. I. Grand Rapids: Eerdmans, reprint edition.

Chafer, Lewis Sperry. *Systematic Theology.* Dallas: Dallas Seminary Press, 1948.

Cole, R. A. *The Gospel According to St. Mark.* Grand Rapids: Eerdmans, 1961.

Earle, Ralph. *Mark: The Gospel of Action.* Chicago: Moody Press, 1970.

Edersheim, Alfred. *The Temple.* Grand Rapids: Eerdmans, Reprinted 1950.

Eusebius. *Ecclesiastical History.* Translated by Hugh Jackson Lawlor and John Ernest Oulton. London: Society for Promoting Christian Knowledge, 1927.

Finegan, Jack. *The Archaeology of the New Testament.* Princeton: Princeton University Press, 1969.

France, R. T. *The Gospel of Mark* in *The New International Greek Commentary.* Grand Rapids: Eerdmans, 2002.

Hendriksen, William. *Exposition of the Gospel According to Mark.* Grand Rapids: Baker, 1975.

Hiebert, D. Edmond. *Mark: A Portrait of the Servant.* Chicago: Moody Press, 1974.

Josephus. *The Jewish War.* Translated by Gaalya Cornfeld. Grand Rapids: Zondervan, 1982.

Kent, Homer A., Jr. *Light in the Darkness.* Grand Rapids: Baker, 1974.

Lane, William L. *The Gospel According to Mark* in *The New International Commentary on the New Testament.* Grand Rapids: Eerdmans, 1974.

Lenski, R. C. H. *The Interpretation of St. Mark's Gospel.* Columbus: Wartburg, 1946.

Loffreda, Stanislao. *Recovering Capharnaum.* Jerusalem: Edizioni Custodia Terra Santa, 1985.

Maclear, G. F. *The Gospel According to St. Mark* in *The Cambridge Bible for Schools and Colleges.* Cambridge: University Press, 1888.

Mann, C. S. *Mark* in *The Anchor Bible* series. Garden City, N.Y.: Doubleday, 1986.

Metzger, Bruce M. *A Textual Commentary on the Greek New Testament.* 2nd ed. New York and Stuttgart: United Bible Societies, 1994.

Moulton, W. F. and A. S. Geden. *A Concordance to the Greek Testament*. Edinburgh: T. & T. Clark, 1950.

Robertson, A. T. *A Harmony of the Gospels*. New York: Harper & Brothers, 1922.

Scroggie, W. Graham. *A Guide to the Gospels*. London: Pickering & Inglis, 1948.

*Student Map Manual*. Edited by James Monson. Jerusalem: Pictorial Archive, 1979.

Swete, Henry Barclay. *The Gospel According to St. Mark*. Grand Rapids: Eerdmans, 1952.

Swift, C. E. Graham. "Mark," *New Bible Commentary*. Grand Rapids: Eerdmans, 1958.

Thomas, Robert L. *Three Views on the Origins of the Synoptic Gospels*. Grand Rapids: Kregel, 2002.

Thomas, Robert L. and F. David Farnell. *The Jesus Crisis*. Grand Rapids: Kregel, 1998.

Thomas, Robert L. and Stanley N. Gundry. *A Harmony of the Gospels*. Chicago: Moody Press, 1978.

Thompson, J. A. "Idumea," *The Illustrated Bible Dictionary*. Leicester, England: InterVarsity, 1980.

Wachsmann, Shelley. *The Sea of Galilee Boat*. New York: Plenum Press, 1995.

Wessel, Walter. "Mark," *The Expositor's Bible Commentary*, Vol. 8. Grand Rapids: Zondervan, 1984.

Wolff, Richard. *The Gospel According to Mark*. Wheaton, Ill.: Tyndale, 1969.

Wuest, Kenneth S. *Mark in the Greek New Testament*. Grand Rapids: Eerdmans, 1950.

## Other Books by Homer A. Kent, Jr.

*The Pastoral Epistles*, Moody Press

*Ephesians, the Glory of the Church (Everyman's Bible Commentary Series)*, Moody Press

*Jerusalem to Rome: Studies in the Book of Acts*, Baker Book House & BMH Books

*The Epistle to the Hebrews*, Baker Book House

*Light in the Darkness: Studies in the Gospel of John*, Baker Book House & BMH Books

*The Freedom of God's Sons: Studies in Galatians*, Baker Book House & BMH Books

*Treasures of Wisdom: Studies in Colossians and Philemon*, Baker Book House & BMH Books

*A Heart Opened Wide: Studies in 2 Corinthians*, Baker Book House & BMH Books

*Faith That Works: Studies in James*, Baker Book House & BMH Books

"Commentary on Matthew," in *Wycliffe Bible Commentary*, Moody Press

"Commentary on Philippians," in *Expositor's Bible Commentary,* Vol. 11, Zondervan Pub. Co.